T0043943

SPYING ON SPIES

HOW ELIZEBETH SMITH FRIEDMAN
BROKE THE NAZIS' SECRET CODES

Elizebeth on her way to testify in federal court, 1934 (George C. Marshall Foundation)

SPYING ON SPIES

· · · · · · · · · · · · · ·

HOW ELIZEBETH SMITH FRIEDMAN BROKE THE NAZIS' SECRET CODES

BY MARISSA MOSS

ABRAMS BOOKS FOR YOUNG READERS • NEW YORK

The illustrations in this book were made with pen, ink, and watercolor wash.

Library of Congress Control Number 2023021301

ISBN 978-1-4197-6731-9

Text and illustrations © 2024 Marissa Moss
Edited by Howard W. Reeves
Book design by Heather Kelly

Printed and bound in U.S.A.
10 9 8 7 6 5 4 3 2 1

Abrams Books for Young Readers are available at special discounts when
purchased in quantity for premiums and promotions as well as fundraising or
educational use. Special editions can also be created to specification. For details,
contact specialsales@abramsbooks.com or the address below.

ABRAMS The Art of Books
195 Broadway, New York, NY 10007
abramsbooks.com

TO THE TRULY BRILLIANT
LISA KABORYCHA,
BECAUSE KNOWLEDGE IS POWER

CONTENTS

• • • • • • • • • • •

ONE

THE MOST FAMOUS CODE-BREAKER IN THE WORLD

Elizebeth may have looked like your average housewife of the time, but in 1934 she was the most famous code-breaker in the world, written up with splashy headlines in magazines and newspapers. A radio reporter at NBC gushed in May that year, "I'll confess, Mrs. Friedman, I was thunderstruck the other day when I met you for the first time. I simply wasn't prepared to find a petite, vivacious young matron bearing the formidable title of crypt-analyst for the US Coast Guard. How did you ever get interested in the highly technical science of codes and crypts?"

Crypts? Elizebeth thought. *Like where you bury people?* She knew the reporter meant "decrypting." But she didn't bother to correct the effusive interviewer. She tried to stay calm and professional, as always.

"I never thought of my job as terribly unusual until the newspapers stumbled upon what I do for the government." She wished they had never found out. Testifying in high-profile criminal cases had suddenly made her a major public figure. Which was exactly what someone who spied on people didn't want. Elizebeth worked every day with important secrets. She wanted to be a secret herself, but the press wouldn't leave her alone.

SPYING ON SPIES

Elizebeth took the telegram that had just been delivered and wrote on the bottom of it, "Ad absurdum!" Each question was more ridiculous than the last. She wasn't going to waste her time answering any of them. Instead, she filed away the request in her growing library of codes and ciphers.

Barbara hadn't expected her mother to answer the telegram. She knew how irritating all this attention was for her. It was more than annoying to Barbara, though. It was scary. Even Elizebeth admitted that "after those smugglers got out of prison, some of them were in very, very mean moods."

Eleven-year-old Barbara knew her mother's work was important. But Elizebeth was often gone, testifying in one major trial after another, facing down vicious mobsters—the kind of mobsters who killed witnesses to keep their mouths shut. Barbara didn't want her mother to be found at the bottom of a river one day.

Even when Elizebeth was home, she spent long hours at her office, often working so late on the many, many messages she needed to decode that her kids didn't see her—or their dad, who had a similar job—for dinner. A nearby restaurant would deliver the meal to them instead. Barbara and her younger brother, John, would eat by themselves. They were used to it.

Elizebeth could see the worry on her daughter's face. "It's OK," she reassured her. "I'm doing exactly what I was meant to do. And you know how hard it was for me to get here."

Barbara did know. Elizebeth had often told her the story of how all this had started. It wasn't a story she shared with reporters, however. It was the story of how a "petite, vivacious" young woman got started in code-breaking. It happened almost twenty years ago, in Chicago of all places, the home of some of the most violent criminals Elizebeth now faced, including the notorious mobster Al Capone.

TWO

A RESTLESS QUESTION MARK

SPYING ON SPIES

Elizebeth Smith had been a stubborn little girl. She was the youngest child of ten in a Quaker family, living in the Indiana countryside. Her father was a dairy farmer. By the time she came along, most of her siblings were out of the house, starting their own lives. Elizebeth felt like nobody expected anything of her, the last one left at home. But she wanted more than being a wife and a mother, the roles most women played in the early 1900s. She felt like a "restless mental question mark," eager for a challenge.

She wanted to broaden her world, to ask a million questions and find some answers. That meant going to college. It was a strange ambition in her family. Only one sister had bothered to study. Her father thought his children should be practical. How did college help farmers, after all?

When her father refused to pay for college tuition, Elizebeth talked him into lending her the money at a steep interest rate of 6 percent. She took in sewing in her dorm room to pay for her expenses. All the scrimping and saving was worth it, though. Her classes opened her mind, introducing her to philosophy, literature, history, and languages. Elizebeth carried her journal with her everywhere, writing down things she noticed, ideas that struck her. She felt like she was getting closer to the answers, to the truth. But she had so many more questions!

She noticed how people used "polite" language to hide the truth. Rather than calling a man "drunk," they would say he was "indisposed." Someone hadn't "died"; they had "passed away." Elizebeth hated this use of flowery language to cloak reality. She thought it was hypocritical. As she wrote in her journal, using such "pretty" words only meant "we glide over the offensiveness of names and calm down our consciences." Elizebeth didn't want to soothe her mind. She wanted to look at the world with critical sharpness. She wanted the bare truth, even if it was ugly, even if it hurt. Maybe especially if it hurt—that made it more interesting!

Elizebeth didn't know it then, but this attitude would turn out to be a big help when she finally found the work she was meant to do. After graduating from college, though, Elizebeth felt like nothing about her was valued. A degree in English in 1915 certainly didn't open any doors for her. Jobs for women were tough to get and mostly meant teaching or nursing. Elizebeth had imagined using language, her knowledge of literature, in some kind of skillful way, but the only work she could find was as a substitute principal at her hometown high school. After a miserable year, Elizebeth quit and left for Chicago, where a college friend lived. She thought she would have more luck finding an interesting job in a big, bustling city.

But day after day after day, nobody would hire her. Women were supposed to get married and raise a family. Period. Elizebeth had other ideas. "I am never quite so gleeful as when I am doing something labeled as an 'ought not.' Why is it? Am I abnormal? Why should something with a risk in it give me an exuberant feeling inside me? I don't know what it is unless it is that characteristic which makes so many people remark that I should have been born a man."

Elizebeth kept knocking on doors, applying for jobs. But at every office she walked into, she was quickly turned away. After days of doors slamming shut on her, she was ready to do the unthinkable. Ready to give up, to go home to her parents and admit she had been wrong to even try for a different life. But before leaving the big city, she decided to give herself one last treat.

Chicago offered a lot of culture, and Elizebeth headed to the Newberry Library, a beautiful building with an entrance like a medieval cathedral. The first thing she noticed was a sign about the collection's rare edition of William Shakespeare's plays. For her, that was like discovering a treasure right next door when she had thought such a thing couldn't be "any nearer to me than the moon."

She headed to where the First Folio was on display, a magnificently large book, printed only seven years after Shakespeare's death. Seeing it filled her with awe, like the feeling "that an archaeologist would have, when he suddenly realized after years of digging that he was inside the tomb of a great pharaoh."

A librarian noticed her quiet intensity, standing so still in front of the book. She asked Elizebeth about her interest in Shakespeare. Elizebeth explained that she had come to the city to find a job, hoping to use her knowledge of English literature for some kind of research. The librarian knew of just the thing! George Fabyan, a wealthy Chicago businessman, often came to admire the First Folio. He thought the book contained secret messages proving that the plays had really been written by Sir Francis Bacon, not by William Shake-speare at all. He'd been looking for an assistant to help crack the code.

Elizebeth had read about the theories questioning the true authorship of Shakespeare's work. She thought they were ridiculous, completely without evidence. But any job was better than going back home a failure.

The librarian rushed off to call Mr. Fabyan. And before Elizebeth had time to think about it, the man himself was there, towering over her. Fabyan was a bear of a man, tall and broad with a thick beard and mustache. He spoke with authority, a wealthy man who was used to being obeyed. "He wasted no time," Elizebeth wrote in her memoir. "He didn't wish to talk to me at the library but at once invited me to his estate . . . and [to] spend the night." Elizebeth was shocked by the offer. She was a single woman and the two had just met, "but he was the kind of man who did not take no for an answer." And she was the kind of woman who liked to take risks.

Still, she objected that she didn't have a toothbrush with her, much less a change of clothes. Fabyan assured her that all "necessaries" would be provided. He whisked her off in his limousine. The car would take them to the Chicago train station. Another car would pick them up at the station in Geneva, Illinois, and take them to River-bank, a large estate complete with laboratories, houses, stables, gardens, a swimming pool, a zoo, even a Dutch windmill that had been taken apart in the Netherlands and rebuilt, piece by piece, in its new home. It was a small village, dedicated to research on a variety of projects. Fabyan explained that he used his vast fortune to explore the unanswered. The Baconian cipher was one of many eccentric obsessions.

Once aboard the train, Elizebeth wondered what she was doing. All the time in the car, she hadn't said a word, while Fabyan had kept up a steady stream of words. She didn't even know the terms of the job being offered. Yet here she was, sitting across from a very large man with an even larger personality. She realized that she "probably appeared a demure little nobody to him."

He leaned toward her, jabbing his nose within inches of her own. "Well," he bellowed, "WHAT DO YOU KNOW?"

Elizebeth leaned back as far as she could. Something hard and fierce sparked in her. It was how she had always coped with bullies. She gave Fabyan a sideways look as she answered with steely quiet, "That remains, sir, for *you* to find out."

Fabyan sat back and roared with laughter, utterly charmed. He wanted someone whip-smart and determined for the job. Elizebeth was exactly the right person.

THREE

THE WORLD OF RIVERBANK

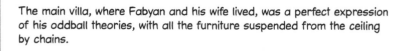

The main villa, where Fabyan and his wife lived, was a perfect expression of his oddball theories, with all the furniture suspended from the ceiling by chains.

The Riverbank Cipher School was intent on proving that Bacon was the real author of the plays attributed to Shakespeare. Fabyan was convinced that the woman leading the work, Elizabeth Wells Gallup, was absolutely right, but she needed help.

At dinner there that first night, Elizebeth met the other "researchers." One young man stood out as the only person close to her own age. William Friedman was neatly dressed in a suit with a bow tie. He sat next to Elizebeth and explained his work on genetics, doing different experiments to improve crop growth.

Elizabeth Wells Gallup was also formally dressed. Elizebeth called her a fine lady, a "real aristocrat." Gallup was a former English teacher and was certain that William Shakespeare was not the real author of all the plays and poems he said he'd written. She had presented her "proof" to visiting professors but hadn't been able to convince them. She needed Elizebeth's help to show more clearly exactly how the Baconian cipher worked in all of the so-called Shakespearean manuscripts. The code was clear proof: hidden statements by Bacon of his authorship.

Elizabeth thought Gallup was lovely, and she was

relieved to have a job, a place to live. But the more she worked on the supposed code, the more she got the sinking feeling that Gallup was absolutely wrong. Instead of proving anything, Gallup was seeing exactly what she wanted to see, finding secret messages that weren't really there.

Elizebeth kept working, though, teaching herself how to analyze and solve codes and ciphers, honing her instincts and noticing patterns. Gallup was no help, but she found a new partner in William, the young man she'd met that first night at dinner. Fabyan asked the young scientist to help with the Baconian cipher project, as well, using his photography skills to enlarge the pages so that looking at the details of the texts would be easier. William, who, like Elizebeth, had no coding background, saw the same problem she did—that there was actually no code at all.

As the two youngest people at Riverbank, Elizebeth and William not only worked together, they spent their free time together. The estate provided bicycles, and they rode all over the three-hundred-acre property, enjoying the strange projects Fabyan funded. There was a giant tuning fork that turned out to be useful for the US military for some top secret reason. Another lab developed a soundproofing material that was used on at least one auditorium's walls. There was no common thread between all the labs. Fabyan had wide interests, from science to literature and history. Most of the projects didn't turn into anything useful, but Fabyan supported them all wholeheartedly. And for some reason, the work on the Baconian cipher project was especially important to him.

Elizebeth just wished it mattered more to her. It all seemed like a silly hoax. With William's support, she decided to focus on real codes and ciphers. She justified this work to Gallup by saying that if she figured out how to crack them, she could bring this knowledge to the Bacon work. What she really hoped was that once she had evidence of what real codes looked like and how they worked, she could convince Gallup there was no actual code hidden in the texts.

Like Elizebeth, William had a sharp, logical mind. Like her, he wanted the truth, no matter what it was. Working with ciphers meant looking for patterns, recognizing the most common letters and letter formations, knowing which words would most likely be used for writing about a particular subject. Both Elizebeth and William had the attention to detail, the focus, and the sheer instinct necessary for solving codes and ciphers. They had also read an enormous amount. Being steeped in language made it easy for them to look at a pattern such as B_G D_G S_ _ _S _TI _ _ and fill in the missing letters: "Big dog sits still."

Supposedly, the Baconian cipher used letter forms to hide meaning. Some letters had serifs, others didn't, and according to Gallup, that was how meaning was hidden in the text. Serif letters are those with little decorative lines sticking out. **This font is serif.** Sans serif letters are cleaner, with no extra lines. This font is sans serif. In the Baconian cipher, a serif letter would be replaced with "b," a sans serif with "a." These sequences of "aaaa" or "aaba" or "aaab" all stood for different letters in the alphabet, which would spell out a secret message. At least Gallup was convinced it did. The message she was finding over and over again was Bacon's claim to be the real author of the plays.

Elizebeth didn't see it quite so neatly. First of all, it wasn't always clear if a letter was serif or sans serif. How can you tell with the letter O, for example? Even more confusing, the printers of the folios used a range of typefaces or fonts, not just two. So interpretation became subjective rather than logical, a no-no for code-breaking. Gallup made the code work for her by interpreting letters in ways that fit her ideas of what she wanted the secret messages to be—the opposite of how code-breaking should work.

Elizebeth and William knew they had to work with the actual text in front of them, not the meaning they wanted to find. The bare truth, as Elizebeth put it, was what really mattered. But Gallup—and Fabyan—refused to listen to them. Even when Elizebeth presented strong arguments disproving any code, Fabyan insisted she was wrong. As Elizebeth said in a later interview, he "wasn't really sincere about the disproving because when any-body tried to convince him that he was wrong, he man-aged to get around them." He was so vocal about Bacon's true authorship that a Hollywood producer sued him in 1916, arguing that Fabyan's loose talk smeared the pro-ducer's planned movies based on Shakespeare's plays.

Astonishingly, the Chicago court sided with Fabyan, believing Gallup's cipher evidence and awarding Fabyan $5,000 in damages, a fortune in those days. Unfortu-nately for Fabyan, he lost the case in a later appeal. Elizebeth thought the whole thing was a publicity stunt, cooked up by the producer, whose name was William Selig, and Fabyan. She had seen the two of them together at Riverbank, talking like old friends. Elizebeth called the lawsuit "a matter of what is properly called collusion."

The movie stunt soured her even more on the Baconian cipher idea. Fortunately, there were plenty of real codes and ciphers for Elizebeth and William to study. If only Fabyan would support that work.

FOUR

THE CIPHER SCHOOL

Despite these frustrations, life was bucolic at Riverbank, a place protected from the outside world. Or so it felt, but the news was getting darker as the world edged toward disaster.

Europe, full of ethnic and nationalistic tensions, was dissolving into all-out war. When an obscure nobleman from Austria-Hungary was assassinated by a Serbian terrorist, Germany and Austria-Hungary declared war on Serbia and its ally Russia. France, Britain, and Belgium were drawn into the fight as Russian allies.

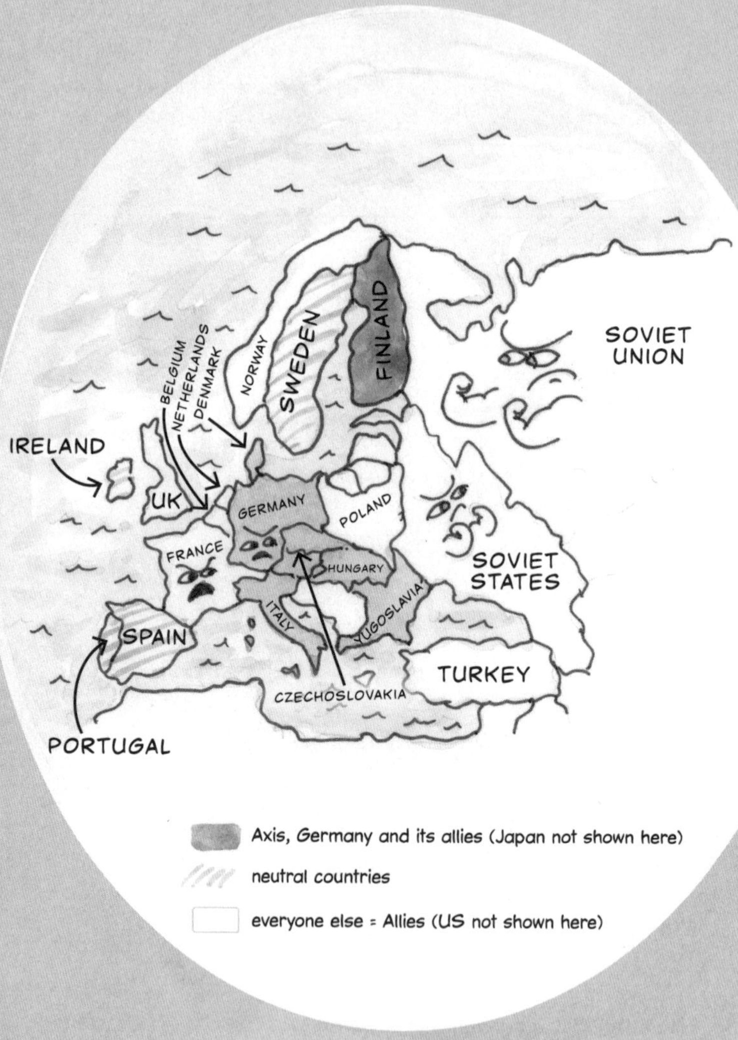

SOVIET
UNION

SWEDEN

FINLAND

NORWAY

BELGIUM
NETHERLANDS
DENMARK

IRELAND

UK

GERMANY

POLAND

SOVIET
STATES

FRANCE

HUNGARY

ITALY

YUGOSLAVIA

SPAIN

TURKEY

PORTUGAL

CZECHOSLOVAKIA

Axis, Germany and its allies (Japan not shown here)

neutral countries

everyone else = Allies (US not shown here)

The United States stayed out of the war, refusing to get entangled in a conflict fought across an ocean for unclear reasons. But Fabyan, with his uncanny talent for predicting future needs, recognized the opportunity that war offered. War meant spies, and spies meant secret codes. Who knew more about codes than members of the cipher school Fabyan had so cleverly founded to crack the Baconian cipher? Elizebeth and William had already paved the way for him with their timely focus on the history of codes.

To broaden their knowledge, Fabyan invited two code experts to speak to his cipher team at Riverbank. The first one was Parker Hitt, who had written the only existing book on military codes and ciphers and was a rare living expert in the field. He couldn't come but sent his wife instead. Mrs. Hitt wasn't a code expert, but she knew how to demonstrate the sliding strip cipher her husband had developed. It was an eye-opening experience for Elizebeth. Here was a real code being shown to her. And a woman was the speaker, not a man. Elizebeth saw the potential right away. Code-breaking was such a new field, there was room for women in it. William was just as excited. He loved his original field of genetics, but this was even more interesting.

SPYING ON SPIES

The second speaker was Joseph Mauborgne, a Signal Corps engineer with the US Army. He had published a book in 1914 about his solution to the Playfair cipher, a coding technique that was easy to use in the field. Messages could be decrypted quickly, using just paper and pencil. Fabyan wasn't as interested in Mauborgne's lecture as having this representative from the Army see how impressive Elizebeth and William were.

His ploy worked. Fabyan pitched his crack team at the cipher school to the War Department. This was before the Central Intelligence Agency (CIA) or the National Security Agency (NSA) or any American intelligence agency existed. Lacking an organization capable of any kind of code-breaking, the War Department sent out a colonel to see what the Riverbank decoders could do. Watching them work, the colonel was impressed with William and Elizebeth (not so much with Gallup, who kept to her work on the Baconian cipher). And Riverbank was secluded, a secure place for top secret work. He recommended that the Army use the cipher school right away. Envelopes full of coded messages and ciphers began to arrive at Riverbank by mail and telegram.

Codes and ciphers were deeply important to the war effort on both sides of the Atlantic. In fact, it was an intercepted code that spurred the United States to finally enter the war, fighting alongside France, England, and Russia against Germany and its allies.

Arthur Zimmerman, a diplomat in the German Embassy in Washington, DC, had sent a telegram to the German ambassador in Mexico. British intelligence intercepted the message, which immediately aroused suspicion since it contained no words but only a series of numbers. Clearly a cipher. Once solved, the message revealed that the Germans were offering Mexico financial support to attack the United States. The plan was that Mexico would distract the Americans from the war in Europe by invading and recapturing their old territories of New Mexico, Arizona, and Texas. It seemed like a great trade-off to the Germans and the Mexicans. This plot revealed Germany as a powerful enemy of the United States. And it was proof that America needed a decryption unit of its own.

Elizebeth and William became that unit. Finally, they could work on actual ciphers and codes, not imaginary ones. They were real code-breakers at last.

FIVE

REAL CODE-BREAKERS

For the first eight months of American involvement in the Great War, later called World War I, Elizabeth and William did all the code-breaking work for the US government. Britain was one of the few countries with an intelligence department, but even theirs was only decades old and tiny. In America, there was no espionage department at all, just a couple of young people with zero military experience.

They send us coded messages with no guides, not even a hint?

That's what decoding means. We've been studying for this.

At least we know there IS a code, unlike the supposed one in Shakespeare's plays.

You know, this is actually a kind of science. Let's call it cryptanalysis.

Figuring out secrets?

Exactly!

From "crypto," Greek for "hidden," and "analysis," Greek for "loosen up," so "cryptanalysis" shakes loose the hidden meaning. The word "cryptography" has similar roots, "crypto" for "hidden" and "graphy" for "writing."

The tiny cipher school did work for the US Army, the US Navy, the State Department, the Department of Justice, the US Post Office, and the Department of Censorship.

SPYING ON SPIES

What's the difference between ciphers and codes? Ciphers replace letters with other letters or symbols. The more complicated ciphers have several different possibilities for each letter, so that "a" could be written as "21" or "143 "or "g," depending on the system used. Old-fashioned decoder rings were actually ciphers.

Codes replace whole words or phrases. Paul Revere used a code, "One if by land, two if by sea," to alert the colonists as to how the British would invade. One beam of light would mean the British were arriving by land, while two flashes would mean a sea arrival. Codes can rely on stock phrases, so "the weather is sunny" could mean "the operation is a go," while "storms ahead" could mean "take precautions."

Both Elizebeth and William found ciphers especially tricky. The only way to solve them was to figure out the machine or key that had created the ciphered message in the first place. To do that, they simply kept at it, for days, weeks, months. They used only paper, pencil, and their brains, until some crack appeared—a single word that made sense, a pattern that emerged, a guess that paid off. And then they would keep digging until they could figure out the system.

The first big case Elizebeth and William cracked wasn't a cipher but a code. They had a pile of messages, a series of numbers only, no letters, from Hindu groups in the United States working with German agents. The Hindus wanted Indian independence from Britain. Germany was encouraging them and offering support so that England would be fighting two battles—one in India and one in Europe. It was the same strategy as the one laid out in the Zimmerman telegram.

That was all they were told. And from that, they needed to figure out what the messages said.

From the groupings of the numbers in the messages, they suspected it was a book code. A particular book was being used as the key to the code. Numbers like 26-12-39 and 4-18-7 suggested the book was one anyone could carry without looking suspicious, since the agent needed to have the book handy. You wouldn't want to carry a book called *Secret Codes*! The first number stood for the page, the second number the line, and the third number the word in the line. So to solve the code in the first example, one would turn to page 26 and look at word 39 in line 12.

Elizebeth tried to guess what the book could be by

learning something about the senders and recipients. The leader in the United States was named Heramba Lal Gupta. His name as a signature was their first clue. They started with the signatures on the messages and worked from there. In this way, they formed a kind of skeleton text, revealing a book about political science and Germany. They knew, for example, that on page 7, line 3, there was the word "constitution." On page 13, line 11, the word "government." In this way, they could decipher the messages even without the right book.

Still, for absolute proof, they needed to find the book used to code and decode. William rummaged through old bookstores and chanced on exactly the right edition of an ordinary book on German politics. With the code completely broken, Elizebeth and William had proof of a plot to take advantage of Britain's attention on the war in Europe to start a violent uprising in India. William testified against the conspirators in a Chicago trial, helping convict fifty plotters.

The second group of Hindus was based on the West Coast and was using a different book. This book probably had columns, since the second number was always a 1 or a 2 (for which column to look in). The column format made Elizebeth and William think of a dictionary. Though both of them cracked the code using the same system they had for the first book, only William was sent to San Francisco to testify about the nature of the code and how it revealed the plots. Elizebeth felt "considerable regret" that she couldn't go, "since we had completed this task completely alone." She was proud of solving this first big case and was curious who these people were, using this clever book code. After working on it in Riverbank for months, it was strange to think these were actual people, working on sabotage that could have had real effects.

Although they had guessed the contents by pattern recognition, Elizebeth and William still hadn't found the exact dictionary used. While William was in San Francisco for the trial, he visited a friend in Berkeley, across the bay, and once again looked in an old bookstore, this time for a German-English dictionary. By another stroke of luck, he found the right one, an old edition dating from 1880. Armed with the book, he could confirm that their decoded messages were 100 percent accurate. But that wasn't the most dramatic moment of the trial.

One of the witnesses was a plotter who had made a deal to testify against his fellow conspirators in exchange for a lighter sentence. William was in court that day, as well. As the traitor got ready to testify, a man in the audience took out a gun and shot him. William watched as a US marshal fired at the assassin, killing him. Once the courtroom calmed down, the trial continued, and all the suspects were convicted.

It was a good thing after all that Elizebeth hadn't come, William told her. This wasn't the kind of actual effects she had been thinking of. Still, Elizebeth would have her chance later to face plenty of angry, vengeful criminals in court.

SIX

A ROMANCE IN CODE

Elizebeth described Fabyan as a loud bully who tried to control all aspects of their lives. "He gave orders on every phase of life, even dictating what clothes I should wear and where I should buy them."

Elizebeth dutifully bought a blouse and a skirt, forced into borrowing the money from Fabyan, who took it out of her already small wages.

William was the opposite of Fabyan. He was gentle, considerate, polite, very handsome.

With William, Elizebeth could say anything. And he didn't tell her how to act or dress or what to say. Instead, he listened.

Fabyan may have been infuriating, but the work he gave them was compelling. It was thrilling to uncover secrets, to solve real cases. Elizebeth loved the work she was doing with William. And she loved spending time with this brilliant young man. William treated her like an equal, someone intelligent. It was a feeling Elizebeth wasn't used to. She'd dated poets and artists in college but nobody since then.

William was different. He clearly cared what she thought and felt. But though they worked long hours together, shared meals and walks, bike rides and jokes, she didn't think of him as a possible boyfriend. As much as she enjoyed his company, she was sure that her hard-nosed determination would deter him—and any man— from thinking of her romantically.

But William loved Elizebeth's stubbornness and quick mind. He was sure that she was the one for him right away. As it dawned on her that he had feelings for her, she didn't know what to think. Brought up as a small-town Quaker, she wasn't sure how she felt about this handsome young man with the warm brown eyes. He was a Romanian Russian Jew whose family had fled anti-Semitism for the safety of the United States. She had never even met anyone Jewish before. His culture and background seemed impossibly foreign. Her parents would certainly never approve. But then, they didn't approve of Elizebeth, anyway.

The more time she spent with William, the more she admired his quick mind, his patience, his kindness, and his sense of humor. She felt like most people were three steps behind her thinking. William kept up. And where other men wanted her to be quiet, he loved listening to her. Where other men tried to control her, he was happy to simply be by her side.

It wasn't a long engagement. As soon as William asked, Elizebeth quickly agreed, and they decided to sneak away from Riverbank to get married on May 17, 1917. A Chicago rabbi married them, with no family or friends attending. They were gone for the weekend only and returned to Riverbank to get right back to solving more ciphers. The only change was that now they shared a room and a last name. Elizebeth kept Smith as a middle name but was happy to take Friedman as her new last name. She'd always considered Smith too ordinary, too much of a cliché. The only thing about her name that was unusual was her mother's insistence on spelling Elizebeth with an *e* in the middle instead of the usual *a* (Elizabeth)—which only made people think she didn't know how to spell. It was an apt name for someone immersed in letters and how they revealed meaning. Elizebeth was no ordinary Elizabeth!

Their honeymoon was spent at Riverbank working on codes. They were in love with each other—and with words, how they could be moved around, changed, and hidden. They wanted to see the secrets nobody else could see. Elizebeth thought she and William were looking more carefully, more deeply, more honestly than most people. Now they'd be doing that together for the rest of their lives.

SEVEN

WHO CAN YOU TRUST?

Most messages in World War I were sent over the radio, which meant anyone could capture or overhear what was being said.

Codes or ciphers were needed to protect the secrecy of important information. For a while, the Army was satisfied sending messages to Riverbank to solve, but as tensions heated up, the US government asked Fabyan to move his cipher school to Washington, DC, where the government could have direct control of the work—and speedier decoding.

Elizebeth and William were so good at their work, the Army sent four young lieutenants to study cryptography with them for several months in the fall of 1917. These men would then go to France, bringing the techniques they learned to the cipher-solving section of General Headquarters for American troops fighting in Europe. Codes, Elizebeth saw, weren't just puzzles. They had real-world impact. They could save lives.

William itched to join the men they had trained. He wanted to serve his country, too. But when he took his Army physical, he failed and was considered unfit to enlist. William was discouraged but believed the diagnosis. Elizebeth did not.

She knew Fabyan was controlling and dishonest. Right away, she suspected that he was behind the bad medical results. She already feared he was intercepting their mail, keeping any job offers away from them. She turned out to be right about both things.

Since William wasn't coming to the Army, the Army came to him. They asked Elizebeth and William to test a cipher machine they wanted to use in the field. It was a British device, the Wheatstone cipher, and supposedly absolutely unbreakable. Elizebeth was in one corner of the room, working on a Spanish message with a translator, when Fabyan brought in a military man with a sheaf of papers, messages from this Wheatstone machine. William worked on the small pile, searching for repetitions, for patterns. After a couple of hours, he called out to Elizebeth, "Would you lean back in your chair and completely relax, and then I'm going to say a word to you and I want you to come back instantly with the first thing that comes into your mind."

Elizebeth leaned back. "'All right, I'm ready.' He said the word 'cipher' and I said 'machine.'"

William was looking for the key word to solve the cipher. He'd figured out one—'cipher'—and was stuck on the second." Elizebeth was exactly right. "Machine" was the second key word. And just like that, the two of them had cracked a supposedly unbreakable cipher.

Naturally, the Army decided not to use the Wheatstone machine. And they wanted William to work for them more than ever.

Fabyan was willing to cooperate only so far with the government. He had brought in more people to work with Elizebeth and William, translators as well as codebreakers. The couple ended up training and working with a small group. This new, expanded unit should have been enough for the War Department—much better than anything the government could do. At least that's what Fabyan thought.

Fabyan was determined to keep a tight rein on all of his code-breakers, making sure they continued to do important work for him alone. That meant not passing on messages or mail from the outside that might take talent away from him. William never heard about the offer of a commission from the Army, something he'd told Elizebeth he wanted. All he knew was that he hadn't passed the physical.

When William didn't respond to the Army, the government knew it couldn't rely on Fabyan anymore. Besides, it didn't make sense to waste time sending messages back and forth. The work had to be done in Washington. So the War Department created its own small Cipher Bureau. Desperate to keep his connections with the government for as long as he could, Fabyan offered to have his crack Cipher School train these inexperienced officers in cryptology. For two months in the winter of 1918, eighty men stayed in town nearby and were taught cryptography and cryptanalysis by Elizebeth and William at Riverbank. When they left, that was the end of the government working with Fabyan. And the end of codes being sent for Elizabeth and William to solve.

By now, William had learned that the War Department had personally requested him. He enlisted as an officer in the Radio Intelligence Unit in the US Army Signal Corps. This time, he mysteriously passed the physical and was sent to France in May 1918. Elizabeth tried to enlist, as well, but as she said, "I, a mere woman, could not follow to pursue my 'trade.'" After all, as a woman, she still couldn't even vote. She felt left out while William continued their important work without her.

Riverbank had been a strange wonderland when Elizebeth first arrived. Now it felt like a cage. Without William around—or any codes to work on except for the silly Bacon project—Elizebeth decided to leave. She sneaked off to the train station without a word and went back home to Indiana. She got a temporary job at the library there and waited impatiently for William to return.

Once the war was over, William stayed in France to work on compiling the codes and ciphers that had been used there. He finally came home in April 1919. The couple tried to figure out where to go, what to do next, but at every job interview, William was passed over. Meanwhile, Fabyan deluged them with telegrams, urging them to come back to Riverbank, promising that they would be paid for the months they'd been away.

Fabyan wrote to Elizebeth, asking to meet with her in person, sure he could convince her that way. He insisted that letters simply couldn't convey his intentions. She responded:

"I am inclined to agree with you that in most cases, correspondence is rather unsatisfactory. But with you . . . it has some advantages—for, you see, in conversation you insist on doing all the talking! Now I suppose you are going to retort, 'This, from a woman?'"

Not only did Elizebeth want to avoid any meeting with Fabyan, she suspected he had reached out to any potential employers and warned them off hiring William. He had that kind of reach and power. And an intense need for control. How else to explain the timing of his persistent telegrams, which always arrived right after one of William's job interviews?

But with no other job offers, William felt they had no choice but to return to Riverbank. At least they would live in town this time, not on the estate. The back pay

Fabyan had promised never materialized, however, and their salary was still pitifully small. "Days, weeks, and months passed by and we were doomed to disappointment," Elizebeth complained.

Soon after their return to Riverbank, the War Department reached out with positions for both Elizebeth and William. When Fabyan heard that, he promised to pay them double what the War Department offered. William wanted to believe Fabyan and convinced Elizebeth to turn down the job. Of course, just as Elizebeth suspected, they never got the increased salary. And now they felt truly stuck. They couldn't go back to the government after refusing them, after all.

At least they didn't have to work on the Baconian cipher anymore. They left that to Gallup, who was as convinced as ever that she was right. Instead, Elizebeth and William documented the work they had done before William left for France.

Elizebeth and William spent their time writing their own guides to cryptanalysis, inventing an entire science. The pamphlets were printed using Riverbank's small press. Fabyan registered the copyrights in his own name—not Elizebeth's, not William's. He went even further by publishing William's first book on cryptography, *The Index of Coincidence*, in France, far from William's eyes, so Fabyan could put his own name on this important work on code-breaking, as well.

Taking credit for the book was one step too far. Elizebeth had long been desperate to leave Fabyan's control. Her father had been an overbearing, imposing man, and Fabyan was just the same, a petty tyrant who kept them in a kind of gilded prison. Now, to her intense relief, William finally agreed with her. They had to escape somehow.

EIGHT

ESCAPE FROM RIVERBANK

Eager to have William back on his team, Mauborgne quickly put together an offer for both William and Elizebeth. They could work for the Army starting on January 1, 1921. William would work with the same officers from the Signal Corps he knew from France. Elizebeth would work for the Signal Corps, as well, helping to create a general system of field codes for the Army. They would do similar work, work together in fact, but as a woman Elizebeth would be paid half of what William would get.

It all sounded fine, but William was afraid of Fabyan and what he would do. He warned Mauborgne that Fabyan was "as powerful as he is ruthless." He would definitely try to derail these new positions, however he could.

To keep Fabyan from stopping them, Elizebeth and William quietly packed up their home and were set to leave as soon as they gave him the news of the Army jobs. They made it clear they had already signed contracts with the government. Forced to admit defeat, "Fabyan accepted his fate, although not in a very gracious manner." Elizebeth kept looking behind her as they left for Washington, sure Fabyan would do something dramatic, something horrible. She relaxed only once they were safely across the country.

SPYING ON SPIES

Elizebeth loved their new home on the outskirts of Washington, DC. Far from Riverbank, she felt she could finally breathe deeply. And she loved working on real codes again. The only thing she didn't love was the Army itself. William was a commissioned officer, a man, so he had status. Elizebeth was a civilian and a woman. She understood her place well. As she described it, "By the end of the war, I was more or less known as a military cipher expert, but I was better known as the wife of my husband." William now cast a big shadow over her, having "made a reputation so startling that I regarded the task of catching up to him as being altogether hopeless."

William didn't feel that way, however. After all, he wouldn't have cracked the Wheatstone cipher machine without her. The two worked together, side by side, exchanging ideas and secrets. It would be the last time they could freely talk about their work with each other. They could share the secrets they worked on.

But Elizebeth wasn't comfortable with the military hierarchy. She knew women weren't welcome, despite having won the right to vote just the previous year. She still couldn't enlist or hold a rank. She was a lowly civilian with "special privileges" that didn't feel so special. Elizebeth knew she had been hired only because she was married to William. So after a year, she quit to stay home, raise a family, and write books.

She started with a book on code-breaking for teens, using lively, fun language to explain different systems. "Miss Transposition Merely Turns Her Clothes Around" meant moving the order of the letters (like an anagram), while "Miss Substitution Changes into a New Outfit" meant replacing letters with numbers or other letters.

After a few months at home, the US Navy offered Elizebeth a position as cryptographer at twice her previous pay. She took it, for once earning as much as her husband, though she knew it wasn't really her they wanted. "This was a case of 'if we can't have William Friedman, we will make use of his brains through his wife.'"

The important position didn't turn out at all as she had expected. Yes, the pay was better, but everything else was much worse. She had no power, no ability to choose her projects. She wasn't solving codes but only creating them. Fed up with being treated like a secretary, Elizebeth resigned six months later, as soon as she had finished the job of setting up a cipher system for the Navy.

Back at home, she started work on another book, an alphabet one this time. She wanted to teach kids about the wonder that simple marks on a page could reveal complicated messages. The alphabet, after all, is a form of code, symbols for meaning. It's the first code we all crack.

And she and William had their first child, a daughter named Barbara. Would Elizebeth become an ordinary wife and mother, after all, as her father had said she should?

NINE

A SPECIAL AGENT

Elizebeth couldn't stay away from codes. Her mind itched for puzzles to solve. So she jumped at the chance to develop a new code when a wealthy businessman approached William for help.

You may have heard of me, Mr. Friedman. I'm the owner and publisher of the *Washington Post*.

Of course, Mr. McLean! What can I do for you?

It's this blasted Teapot Dome business! Has all of us spooked, worried about the law poking its nose into our private business.

The Teapot Dome scandal was all over the front pages.

FINANCIAL FRAUD

SLUSH FUND FOR OIL COS. GUILTY!

BRIBES PAID!

EMOLUMENT SALE

Coded messages—deciphered by William—had proved that the secretary of the interior, Albert Fall, had taken a bribe to arrange for cheap leases of government land with oil reserves to private companies. Fall was convicted and sent to prison, and the reputation of President Harding was seriously damaged.

William accepted the job, but being busy with the Army, it was Elizebeth who did the actual work. In echoes of the problems with Fabyan, another fabulously rich man who was very stingy with money, McLean didn't pay William or Elizebeth for their work once the code had been delivered.

Elizebeth wanted to complain loudly enough to embarrass the businessman. William refused, worried that he'd look like a "money-grubbing Jew." The 1920s was a time of heightened anti-Semitism, and William was keenly aware of how his colleagues already looked at him with suspicion. The military he worked for had files with titles like "Jews: Race," "Jewish Question," and "The Power and Aims of International Jewry." Harvard no longer accepted Jews as students. Many job listings stated bluntly: "Christians only." Henry Ford made every Ford dealer in the country stock piles of an ugly anti-Semitic tract about how evil Jews were trying to take over the world in a vast global conspiracy.

Elizebeth still felt William should speak up. William had grown up with his family's stories of violent hatred toward Jews. He didn't want to provoke a reaction or risk losing a job he loved. Elizebeth had never seen how vicious people could be toward Jews. She didn't understand how deep-seated anti-Semitism was, how easily stirred up. She would see that herself all too soon.

It took two years for McLean to pay the bill he owed. Elizebeth swore she wouldn't work for a wealthy patron ever again.

Would she work for *anyone* again? Or would she focus on her baby and write children's books instead? As Barbara started to talk, Elizebeth couldn't help herself—she analyzed the baby babble like a code-breaker, looking for patterns, searching for words in the sounds.

Elizebeth was simply too good at breaking codes to quit doing it. Different agencies kept asking her to work for them. Elizebeth thought it wasn't really her they wanted. As she later explained, different departments would try to hire William away from the Signal Corps, "and when they couldn't get him, I'd be offered a job. So I said rather bitterly sometime recently . . . That's the story of my life. Somebody asks for my husband and they can't get him, so they take me."

In 1925, after a year at home, Elizebeth was approached by the Justice Department. The Coast Guard had collected hundreds of coded messages from criminal gangs, and there was nobody who could solve them. Elizebeth hesitated, worried about a situation like at the Navy, one with an illusion of control but without any real power. Still, the lure of the puzzles was too strong. Studying baby talk wasn't as interesting as she'd hoped. She agreed, so long as she could work from home. A live-in housekeeper would help with two-year-old Barbara. Far from the military hierarchy, Elizebeth could work in peace and still be with her family. Another baby was coming later that year.

The Justice Department wanted Elizebeth to catch rumrunners, criminal gangs who were smuggling booze into the United States. It was big business once the Volstead Act of 1919 had made the sale and distribution of alcoholic beverages illegal in the United States.

Elizebeth was given a metal badge that read "Special Agent, US Treasury" in gold letters, since Treasury agents were charged with enforcing Prohibition. Every week, she picked up a new batch of messages from the Treasury Building. She brought them back solved the following week. In the first three months, working at her kitchen table, she cracked two years' worth of messages and cleared up the Coast Guard's backlog. She was wading deep into complicated criminal networks. This was a time when the Federal Bureau of Investigation (FBI) was weak and inefficient. Instead, T-men, or Treasury Men, were the major crime fighters. Al Capone, the brutal Chicago mobster, and Bruno Hauptmann, the kidnapper of the baby of the famous aviator Charles Lindbergh, were both caught by T-men. Elizebeth and her code-cracking skills became an important tool for catching violent criminals.

Though she had started with the Justice Department, she ended up cracking codes for five other agencies, as well—the US Treasury, US Coast Guard, Bureau of Narcotics, Bureau of Internal Revenue, and Bureau of Prohibition and Customs. She paused to give birth to a son, John Ramsey, and got right back to code-breaking. It was simply part of who she was. She didn't want to cut down on her long hours or all the travel she'd been doing. Instead, she hired a nanny who came at seven in the morning and left at seven at night. Barbara was still cared for by the live-in housekeeper.

As the only senior cryptanalyst at the Treasury, Elizebeth also worked with agents in the field and helped train T-men so they knew where to aim their radios to intercept messages, directing them to where she knew the smugglers were working. In 1928, she spent time on the West Coast to instruct the Coast Guard agents there about the criminal gangs in their waters. "I went here, there, and everywhere I was needed," she noted. She enjoyed going to Houston, New Orleans, and San Francisco on airplanes, a new way to travel across the country. This was a time when flights were mainly for businessmen, and she was usually the only woman on the plane—such an oddity that the pilot often came out to chat with her, wondering who this female passenger could be.

It was all great fun for Elizebeth, but this was the period when her young daughter worried most about her. "It scared me to death," Barbara said. Between 1920 and 1933, ninety-seven Treasury agents were killed in the line of duty. Barbara wondered if her mother's tin badge was worth the risk. Elizebeth had no doubts.

TEN

CODES AT HOME

Elizebeth didn't just work on codes—she lived her life in code. With or without an official position, codes were intertwined with how she thought.

The family sent out Christmas cards in code, complicated inventions including photos of William, Elizebeth, Barbara, and John.

Some codes involved numbers, some letters, and others were completely visual, so that whether a person faced forward or to the side revealed the message.

The visual code worked like the Baconian cipher, with facing forward representing a serif letter and facing sideways representing a sans serif one. After all, the serif, sans serif idea simply meant you needed two kinds of formats.

So if serif = a in the Baconian cipher, then sans serif = b. In this picture, let's say that profiles = serif = a and full-face = sans serif = b.

Then this picture shows:
babbba bbaba abba

Or in the Baconian units of 5:
babbb abbab aabba

Which in the Baconian cipher =
babbb = Z
abbab = O
aabba = G

Which spells out ZOG and then the receiver needs to guess what the initials could stand for. We don't know. Do you?

SPYING ON SPIES

In 1928, the Christmas code-card was a "turning grille," a square of red paper with circular holes. The four sides were numbered 1 through 4. The numbering let the recipient know that they should turn the square counterclockwise. This square was set over the accompanying coded letter and the message was read through the holes. The first side showed: "FOR CHRISTMAS GREETINGS IN 28 [1928]." After a ninety-degree turn, side two read: "WE USE A MEANS QUITE UP TO DATE." The third turn revealed: "A CRYPTO TELEPHOTOGRAM HERE." The final turn: "BRINGS YOU WORD OF CHRISTMAS CHEER."

Elizebeth and William hosted puzzle dinner parties where guests had to crack codes to figure out the address of the restaurant where they should go for the first course and then had to solve another cipher for the main course. The most complicated cipher was saved for dessert, of course. You had to work hard to earn the treat!

For dinners at home, guests would be handed a menu—in code, naturally—and urged to guess what would be served. One was a series of blue dots, which stood for blue point oysters. The codes Elizebeth and William faced at work were serious, often dangerous, but those at home were full of fun.

When the family got a dog, an Airedale terrier, it was named Crypto, of course. When the children got older, they wrote postcards home from camp in code, matching the coded messages they got in turn from their parents. Her first time away at camp, Barbara wrote home in an easy transposition cipher (just move down one letter so A = B, B = C, etc.): EFBS NPUIFS BOE EFBS EBEEZ. When Elizebeth and William were in Madrid for a big cryptography conference in 1932, Barbara wrote them messages in a more complicated cipher. Codes were woven into the family's everyday lives, part of how they saw the world, how they moved through it.

Barbara wanted to be a professional dancer when she grew up, but her brother, John, was already set on being a code expert like his parents. Both kids were avid players of the coding game their father was developing. He called it *Kriptor* and hoped to sell it to Milton Bradley, the company that made *Battleship* and *The Game of Life*. Players would be either a "code-maker" or a "code-breaker" and would trade secret messages.

Dinner table conversations were often about codes,

but the simple kinds the parents could explain to their children. They wanted Barbara and John to see coding as fun.

Work for Elizebeth and William, however, was a totally different sort of coding. It was not simple play and created the tension of keeping secrets from the person they wanted to share them with most. There were times when their projects overlapped, but William's Army work was usually too secret for Elizebeth to know about. They could talk about codes in general, but the days of sharing work stories and problems were over. Elizebeth could talk about some of her cases, especially after they had been solved and gone to trial. But William had to stay quiet. It was an enormous strain on him—and on most of the people who worked in his unit.

Playing with codes at home helped relieve the stress for the whole family. And for Elizebeth, it was simply how her mind worked, something she couldn't shut off.

ELEVEN

THE KEY WOMAN OF THE T-MEN

Prohibition was a major source of the crime Elizebeth tracked. What was being prohibited was the sale of all alcohol through a constitutional amendment.

The law was widely ignored, with a large portion of the population drinking in secret bars called speakeasies or getting a doctor's prescription for "spirits." The underground market for alcohol was so big, it even included lawmakers.

Elizebeth wrote that buying illegal liquor "was reported to be very common in the halls of Congress." In New York City alone, more than 15,000 people a month were arrested for dealing in alcohol. When cases went to trial, the criminals were usually acquitted by sympathetic juries. In San Francisco, Elizebeth noted, "a jury itself was tried for drinking up the evidence."

There was a lot of money at stake with these crimes. Elizebeth explained that "Al Capone was said to make from fifty to one-hundred million dollars a year from beer alone." And these were 1920s dollars, worth almost two billion dollars today! The codes Elizebeth faced now were much more sophisticated than those she'd solved in the First World War. There was a lot at stake. Plus the smugglers were savvy and knew they were being overheard. There was so much criminal activity, so many messages, there was no way Elizebeth could solve all of them. One month alone brought in a pile of 2,000 messages!

Elizebeth begged for a team to help her. She was allowed to hire only one woman, a clerk typist. Still, she managed to solve 12,000 messages between 1926 and 1929, tracking criminal rings from the Pacific to the Atlantic, all the way to the Bahamas. Using the techniques she and William had developed, code-breakers could solve codes in any language. Elizebeth cracked codes in Chinese, Portuguese, Spanish, French, Czech, and German. Sometimes she used a translator to help, but often she simply relied on dictionaries and her own intuitions about how language works.

With the stock market crash of 1929, liquor sales

rose even more. Although most of the country was plunged into high unemployment and a tremendous loss of income, there were enormous fortunes to be made in alcohol smuggling. This meant more crime, more secret messages about it, and more court cases. Elizebeth's days grew even longer. She started work before her children woke up and finished long after they went to bed.

Elizebeth felt crushed by the workload. She kept asking for help. Finally in 1930, the Treasury Department allowed Elizebeth to hire and train a small team of cryptanalysts and cryptographic clerks. The new unit was housed with the Coast Guard, to be closer to where the radio intercepts were made—messages could be quickly passed down the hall instead of to another building. This site served all the law enforcement agencies under the Treasury.

Now that Elizebeth had an office to run, there was no more working from home—not that she was home for her children, anyway. But Barbara and John didn't know any other kind of parent. Both their mother and their father were obsessed with secret codes and spent long days solving them. To the kids, this was simply normal life.

It was normal life for Elizebeth, as well, though she

was relieved to have a group working under her. With the added responsibility came a pay raise and a new title, a first for a woman: cryptanalyst-in-charge, US Coast Guard. It was a title Elizebeth was proud to have.

Elizebeth was often asked later what it was like to hire, train, and manage a group of men. She was relieved that she could honestly say it had worked out well:

> I must declare with all truth that with one exception, all of the men, young or older, who have worked for me and under me and with me, have been true colleagues and have never been obstructionists in any way. I recall particularly that just before World War II . . . I trained four noncommissioned Coast Guard officers . . . These men were not young. When they were leaving at the end of their course, they took particular pains to inform me that when they had received their orders to report to my office . . . they had great misgivings, but that the two years training had been one of pleasure and benefit and profit in every way.

There was sexism, to be sure, but it rarely came from her colleagues. Instead, it came from the press when they reported about the cases she was involved in. The days of William testifying in court were long over now that his work was top secret. Now it was Elizebeth who traveled the country, facing down some of the most violent criminals of the time. She often went to the trials with an armed escort to protect her, the only woman in the courtroom aside from the court stenographer.

In one of her cases, a suspect was killed and two Treasury agents were shot. Elizebeth was warned that the defendants were in a "very mean mood" and she needed a larger security detail than usual. She thought reporters should focus on that, not on the fact she was a woman.

But an expert female witness in these violent cases was itself considered big news. Reporters saw her as completely out of place, a fascinating curiosity. Newspapers described her as the slender woman who knew all the secrets. *Reader's Digest* called Elizebeth the "Key woman of the T-men . . . entrusted with more secrets of the crime world and of federal detection activities than any woman in history." A radio report included her as one of the "First Ladies of the Capitol." Elizebeth was now far more famous than her husband. For her, that wasn't a good thing. She hated all the attention. She didn't think a woman should be a major headline just for being smart. Nor did she appreciate being described as "a pretty young woman in a frilly pink dress."

But what she really resented were the bald-faced lies. She wrote, "One of the fictions which somewhere, somehow, first appeared as a statement and then was perpetuated thereafter in a manner most annoying to me and which must have been extremely annoying to my husband, was the idiotic statement that I, this 'wizard of codes and ciphers,' had taught the science to my husband. Of all the unfounded statements made concerning me in the press, this was the most confounding."

William, however, was the first to say how much he relied on Elizebeth. He wrote to her on one of his trips, "I know how much I owe to you—for love, for wisdom, for courage, and common sense." They were both brilliant code-crackers, but William was moodier. In 1930, he started working on Japanese diplomatic codes, making him feel even more crushed by the weight of the secrets he carried. He was careful not to say a word to his wife, though she could read the code in his face when he was under a lot of strain. Those were the days when he slept in the spare room, afraid he would mumble something as he slept. Barbara described, "Dad used to joke about how they were forced to sleep in separate bedrooms in case they talked about each other's work . . . it was national security."

It was a joke with a sharp bite to it. Elizebeth supported him as best she could. William later said that Elizebeth healed him, that her "own indomitable spirit helped me climb up out of a psychological morass that was pretty deep and distressing."

For Elizebeth, code work was thrilling and exciting. The media attention was annoying, but as William noted, nothing could crush Elizebeth. She stared down gum-chewing lawyers and violent criminals with the same steely look she'd once given Fabyan long ago on the train to Riverbank.

TWELVE

CATCHING CRIMINALS

While William listened to military messages, Elizebeth listened to criminals. She was the one in the public eye, testifying at high-profile trials.

She tried to explain as little as possible about how the codes worked. She hated the way the press wrote about her, as if it was amazing that a woman had a brain, and constantly worried they gave away too many tradecraft secrets to the enemy.

The tough part about cracking secret messages was making sure the enemy didn't know you could read them in the first place.

You had to weigh acting on the information you'd learned against giving away how the spying had been done. Because once the enemy knew that a code or cipher had been cracked, they would use a new one.

And the cryptanalyst would have to start all over again.

SPYING ON SPIES

The perfect balance for Elizebeth, for any code-cracker, was to listen in on secret messages, pass on the information, and learn all you could about the enemy—all while trying to find other ways the information could have been gotten so that the enemy would think somebody had talked, been sloppy, left a clue, anything except that their code had been cracked. Solving the code or cipher was a deep thrill for Elizebeth, every time. This was what she'd always wanted, something that presented a new challenge each day.

In May 1933, Elizebeth went to New Orleans to testify in a giant conspiracy case. There were twenty-three suspects on trial, agents of the Consolidated Exporters Corporation. It sounded like an ordinary business, but it was a criminal operation that smuggled alcohol on eight ships in the Gulf of Mexico. The head of the operation and his three codefendants were all associates of Al Capone, the notorious Chicago mob boss. One was Capone's brother. Elizebeth described them as "about the most disreputable looking men you would ever want to see." These criminals were so violent that Elizebeth once again was assigned security guards to protect her. This gang was well-known for killing "snitches" or anyone else who got in their way.

When Capone's lawyer, Edwin Grace, questioned Elizebeth, he mocked her code solutions as complete inventions. So Elizebeth asked for a blackboard to be brought in and for once clearly explained how she'd cracked the meaning. One newspaper headline blared, "Class in Cryptology," making Elizebeth cringe. She hadn't wanted to give away any trade secrets but had to prove the scientific basis of her work. She needed the men on trial to be safely behind bars. And thanks to her testimony, that's what happened.

After Prohibition—the Volstead Act—was repealed at the end of 1933, Elizebeth continued to track drug and arms smuggling. One thing Prohibition had been supremely effective at was creating criminal networks. These gangs didn't disappear once alcohol was legal again. Instead, they just changed the products they sold—guns and drugs instead of booze. And there was a backlog of old criminal cases that still had to go to trial.

Elizebeth continued to testify in high-profile cases. Each time, she had a security detail assigned to her just in case things got ugly. Just as unnerving was the uncertainty about how long these things would take, from the first deciphering of messages to the court appearances. She wrote, "I pack my bag and hug my children a good bye, which is to last for a week or a month or longer, I know not, and board a train with a prayer that the new fields to conquer will not be impossible."

Conquer she did, sending one criminal network after another to prison. When she was asked how she broke the code of a big drug cartel from Shanghai, she insisted, "We have to keep our ideas secret so that we don't give other smugglers any new ideas." She tried to direct attention to the Coast Guard, the T-men, away from herself, but she recognized that being a woman gave the news stories extra appeal: "The mystery-lure of the words code and cipher, coupled with a woman's name, invariably inflames the reporters and they start on the trail of a story."

In one famous case, the Royal Canadian Mounted Police asked Elizebeth for help cracking the code of a Chinese businessman in Vancouver. Supposedly dealing in gems, Mr. Lew Kim Yuen actually made his fortune by smuggling large amounts of opium. Elizebeth used her familiarity with business codes and abbreviations to crack a code in Chinese, a language she couldn't read. "I argued to myself that the Chinese have a very set mind and a very traditional and what you might say formal way, about everything they say; it's all done in such a fixed pattern." Since these were commercial messages, she looked for certain phrases such as "please reply," "send money at once," and "rush order." A Chinese translator who was brought in confirmed that Elizebeth's hunches were right.

Not only could Elizebeth prove that drugs were being smuggled, but the coded messages revealed how they got to shore. First, they were hidden in hollow posts on the ship's decks. The posts were sawed open, and the drugs, wrapped up like little bales of cotton, were tied together with a rope and lowered into the hollow posts, which were then sealed again. When the ship got to be a mile from shore around Seattle, a mobster would swim out to the ship. While he treaded water, the rope with all the drugs would be removed from the posts and lowered to him. The man would then swim back to shore, dragging the rope between his teeth. It was a clever—and difficult—way to avoid a customs search.

With such dramatic details, Elizebeth couldn't escape the glare of media attention. NBC Radio interviewed her about her work in 1934. The February 15, 1938, issue of *Look* featured "outstanding" women "in careers unusual for their sex." The article included a deep-sea diver, a conductor, a silversmith, and a cryptanalyst—Elizebeth.

Elizebeth had wanted to be as successful at code-breaking as William, but this wasn't at all what she had meant by that.

THIRTEEN

WAR AGAIN?

Armies have always needed to send messages. In ancient times, riders on horseback would carry communications between troops and generals. Homing pigeons were also used, then flags, which could be seen at a distance. With the invention of the telegraph by Samuel Morse in the 1830s, messages could be sent far greater distances, and more quickly, by using Morse code communicated through telegraph wires.

I'm a secret agent!

You look like a stool pigeon!

By World War I, the radio allowed the same thing without the wires. It was much more efficient than telegraphs but was also much more easily overheard. Any radio operator tuned to the right frequency could listen in. Radio made codes essential in the war.

Maybe this?

Or this?

You're getting it!

Both to make and to break.

Anna Smith Strong, one of the spies in George Washington's Culper Ring, used laundry as a signal to the colonists fighting the British. A black petticoat on the line meant there was a message to pick up, and the handkerchiefs next to it indicated where the message was hidden.

I see three handkerchiefs—it's the third cove after the bay!

Heading there now!

Other codes were used in the Civil War. The Freemason's Cipher was popular. The alphabet was put into either a grid or within diagonals and then instead of using the letters, the writers would use the shapes around the letters, with dots to distinguish the grids.

⌐ ⌐· ⌐ < ·⌐· ⌐⌐ □ > □ ⌐ ∨

A	B	C
D	E	F
G	H	I

J.	K.	L.
M.	N.	O.
P.	Q.	R.

	S	
T	U	...
	V	

	W	
X	.	Y
	Z	

A = ⌐   W = ∨
B = □   O = ⌐·
C = L   P = ·⌐

When Allan Pinkerton wrote to his partner at the Pinkerton Agency that President-Elect Abraham Lincoln had made it safely to the inauguration in Washington, DC, despite a planned assassination attempt, his message read: "Plum has nuts." "Plum" was Pinkerton. Who would "nuts" be?

Once again, the United States wasn't eager to enter a war in Europe, but the government needed to know what was going on. And that meant listening to spies by breaking their codes. President Franklin Delano Roosevelt worried about Nazi influence in South America. Nobody had forgotten how the Germans had tried to ally with Mexico during World War I, hoping to distract the United States from the conflict in Europe by starting one with Mexico instead. The connections to South America now were even deeper than during the First World War. So many Germans had fled to South America since then that there were more than two hundred German-language schools in Argentina alone. A fifth of Brazil's population was German. President Roosevelt feared the Nazis would use these connections to try the same tactic again, encouraging Japan and South American countries to attack the United States.

At the end of 1938, Elizebeth still worked with her unit at the Coast Guard under the direction of the Treasury Department. But now she followed a vast network of Nazi spies. Elizebeth spoke about her decrypting work during the Great War and Prohibition, but other than bland generalities, she would never say anything about her government work after that. Neither her unpublished memoir nor later interviews ever ventured into that realm. She only said that she did "the spy stuff!" But the secrecy was oppressive, "a vast dome of silence from which I can never return." She was now firmly in spy work—counterespionage actually, spying on enemy spies.

This only made Elizebeth even more anxious when reporters continued to sensationalize her work. One story in the 1939 *Miami Herald* was particularly worrying. Elizebeth was furious with the headline: "The Woman All Spies in U.S. Fear: How the Amazing Cryptanalyst Uncle Sam Has Ready to Tell Him What Foreign Spies Are Putting into Their Secret Messages Does Her Work." She was even more outraged by how the story ended: "The fame of Mrs. Friedman as a nemesis of plotters has gone around the world and secret agents will be extra careful to prevent giving her a chance to bare their handiwork."

Elizebeth was so upset, she complained to the assistant Treasury secretary about the sloppy press endangering national security: "It is a hodge-podge of plagiarism pulled from here, a bit from there, the whole misinterpreted and sensationalized to give color to the red-flag word SPIES . . . I had nothing to do with espionage trials, as you know." She added: "I'm angry enough over the matter to lobby for a law making it libel for the press even to use the name of a government employee without written consent of that person and the department wherein employed."

The Treasury thought it best not to add fuel to the flames, to simply ignore such stories, but they issued new rules that any employees working on espionage and counterespionage were not allowed to give public testimony. This was a big relief. No more testifying at trials! Now Elizebeth could focus on the work that really mattered: spying on spies.

After the war, Elizebeth would describe this work generally as "exciting, round-the-clock adventures, as we counter-spied into the minds and activities of the agents attempting to spy into those of the United States."

Elizebeth's unit mostly listened to Nazi spies head-quartered in sympathetic Argentina, but there were agents throughout South America. At first, the spies used old-fashioned book codes, the kind where the message is a series of numbers referring to pages, lines, or words in a specific book. Elizebeth and her team solved these quickly. Then the codes got more complicated, using the grid method. And then they got yet more complicated, using the Enigma machine, an encoding device developed in Germany at the end of World War I. This new version of Enigma was more sophisticated than anything ever seen before.

William was working on solving something equally challenging: the cipher machine used by the Japanese, allies of Germany. This system was nicknamed "Purple" and was based on a machine similar to the German Enigma. Both of these machines looked like typewriters attached to rotors. The rotors would be turned to a specific setting and the message would be typed on the regular keyboard. As the letters were pressed, other letters, the encoded version, would light up. These lit-up letters would be written down and become the enciphered message. Only someone with the same machine who knew the right position of the rotors could decipher the message. It was devilishly difficult, since there was an almost infinite number of possibilities—two hundred million variations. This was the machine that both Elizebeth and William had to crack.

Now they were both working on top-secret stuff, on the same kind of cipher machine, though they didn't know it. Elizebeth said dinners at home were quiet, each one afraid of letting something slip. "It gets mixed up in your mind as to what you can talk about safely, and to whom . . . You tend to feel that the easiest thing to do, or the safest thing to do, is just not talk . . . Just never, never say anything."

Elizebeth could manage this. It was harder for William.

FOURTEEN

ENIGMA, THE IMPOSSIBLE MACHINE

Polish mathematicians had been the first to figure out the original German Enigma machine from the First World War. In 1932, Polish intelligence used algebra to solve these early versions. They passed these solutions on to the British and the Americans, along with early models of the "bombe," an electro-mechanical machine (a proto-computer) used to reverse engineer the Enigma ciphers.

Enigma machine— "enigma" means "difficult puzzle, impossible to solve."

→ rotors with letters
→ keyboard with letters
→ plugboard with letters

Alan Turing and his code-breaking team at Bletchley Park in England built a much more complicated and effective bombe to crack the later, more sophisticated Enigma machines by using pattern recognition.

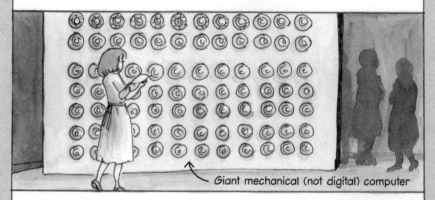

↖ Giant mechanical (not digital) computer

But neither Elizabeth nor William had these early calculator machines. They had to crack Enigma by amassing enough messages to spot repetitions. Which is exactly what they did.

In September 1940, Gene Grotjan, a young woman on William's team, was the first to identify a subtle cycle of repetition in the Japanese Purple code. That foothold was all the team needed to crack the machine, using only paper and pencils. By the end of the month, they had fully deciphered the first message. Using that knowledge, they could reverse engineer a Purple machine. William built their own ramshackle Enigma Purple machine out of odds and ends. Then his team used the makeshift machine to solve thousands of messages. The first words of the code would let the recipient know how to set the rotors on the machine. After that, it was just a question of inputting the encrypted text and seeing what came out. These top-secret decoded messages were called "Magic" and were sent off to the Army and the Navy. The trick, of course, was to use insider knowledge to save lives without tipping off the enemy that their code had been cracked.

William couldn't tell Elizebeth exactly what his team had done, but she saw the toll the work took on him. She later admitted that the one time he had mentioned anything about his secret work was in connection with Purple. One day, Mauborgne, the chief signal officer, called William into his office and said, "Look, this group that I have working on the Japanese cipher are getting nowhere. I want you to drop everything and devote your entire time to that." Elizebeth stressed that was all William had told her:

> He didn't mention what was going on or what machines were known to be in existence or anything. And the thing that astounds me so, as I've looked back on it many times, was that the day that the first messages, when they made that Purple machine . . . out of nuts, bolts, screws, rusty this and that, pieces of everything and they got the machine to the point where he ran a message through it . . . now wouldn't you have thought that any being that was human couldn't have resisted? That they would have said something on that day? Never said a word to me. I didn't know anything about it.

Elizebeth later recognized what a big success this was—that William had managed to reverse engineer the Japanese cipher machine on the basis of the messages alone. She remembered one day when he came home from work with a new lightness around him. She figured that must have been when the breakthrough happened.

Barbara had a similar memory from that time. She knew "he had done something important because he seemed so elated, so triumphant." This was her last year at home before leaving for college in New York. John had been living at a prep school in Pennsylvania for years, so he missed this rare event.

Elizebeth later learned that William's "makeshift machine . . . worked better and faster than the honest-to-god Purple machine when they finally got hold of a real Purple machine." But again, this wasn't something William could tell her at the time.

These were days when William worked even longer hours than usual. Both he and Elizebeth worked so late that often Barbara would not see them for days. As Barbara described it, they both worked six days a week, nine-to-ten-hour days. "They were gone long before I came down to have breakfast." William would come home to collapse into bed, only for Elizebeth to find him up again in the middle of the night. "Sometimes I'd awaken and find him down in the kitchen making a Dagwood sandwich at three o'clock in the morning."

SPYING ON SPIES

All the stress took its toll. A few months after figuring out Purple, on January 4, 1941, William didn't come home from work at all. Instead, he checked himself into Walter Reed General Hospital. He told the doctor that he had collapsed a few days earlier. He'd kept that secret from Elizebeth, as well. But now he worried that he was having a nervous breakdown. The strain of solving Purple, of keeping so many secrets, led him to be hospitalized. Elizebeth came to visit every day, but there was no privacy in the large room shared by all the patients in the neuropsychiatric section. She told William how much she loved him, but they couldn't talk about his work or hers, his worries, or hers. Working on secrets, they never could.

When William tried to return to active duty that spring, the Army gave him an honorable discharge for "reason of physical disqualification." His rank wasn't restored until 1946, though he was so valuable that he continued his decryption work as a civilian, just as Elizebeth had always done. Both of them were too vital to be shut out of government work, with or without military status. They both kept on cracking codes. And lived with the heavy burden of secrecy.

For William, this compartmentalization was trickier. That was part of what had caused his mental collapse in the first place. He couldn't turn off his brain the way Elizebeth seemed to be able to do. Instead he came home still thinking obsessively about Japanese codes and their plans to expand their empire. Having cracked Purple, William's team made two more Purple machines to give to the British at Bletchley Park, the top-secret locale where that country's code-breakers were stationed. It was the beginning of a US—Bletchley Park exchange of information, though Turing's team didn't offer any of their insights into the Germans' Enigma machine.

If William could have shared his worries, his excitement, his hunches with Elizebeth, it would have been much easier. Elizebeth supported him as best she could— by not asking any questions. Naturally, she wondered what he was learning, but she had her own spies to track. And a new job on top of that one.

J. Edgar Hoover, the head of the FBI since 1935, considered women so incompetent that he fired the two female agents at the organization as soon as he took over and made it official policy not to hire any new ones. Still, he turned to Elizebeth to train the staff of the FBI's new cryptographic unit. He felt he had no choice. He figured he would use Elizebeth only to get his own unit up and running. He didn't really need her. He was just using her for a short time.

But when this new unit couldn't break the coded messages the FBI had collected, Hoover had to turn to Elizebeth again. This time, he asked her to help with a spy the FBI had been watching for more than a year. The man, Frederick "Fritz" Joubert Duquesne, was a master spy, skilled at spotting and losing the FBI agents tracking him. He communicated with his agents using a sophisticated code. Unless they could read these messages, the FBI would have no idea what the spies were doing. And without the decrypted messages, they would have no evidence to arrest and convict them. The FBI had one advantage, though: a double agent. William Sebold warned the agency of the scale of Duquesne's operation— thirty-two Nazi agents, all on American soil. These high numbers alone made stopping them a top priority.

By the summer of 1941, Elizebeth and her unit had decrypted hundreds of messages between Duquesne; his spies in America; and Nazi agents in South America, Mexico, and Germany. The messages were a gold mine of information about spies in other countries, as well as providing essential evidence.

On June 28, 1941, the FBI swept up the entire spy ring, the biggest espionage case ever in the United States. Nineteen of the spies pleaded guilty right away. The rest went on trial and all were found guilty and sent behind bars. Duquesne, who had escaped prison twice before, was finally locked away. His spying days were over.

The trial was a big public relations coup for the FBI, a huge success that discouraged future Nazi spies in America. But to Elizebeth, it was evidence of sloppy FBI strategies. During the very public trial, "the FBI exposed the secret messages and methods without as much as asking a by-your-leave from the Treasury Department [the place] where the solutions and systems were achieved." Hoover could have the credit—he just shouldn't have given away the spy-craft.

Elizebeth would never trust Hoover again.

FIFTEEN

THE UNITED STATES—AND ELIZEBETH—IN THE WAR

Elizebeth and William were working on the same thing again, both as civilians, only in two different agencies. Elizebeth continued to head up her *Coast Guard* unit. William, recovered from his breakdown, worked with the Army. Though they were both solving secret messages, once again, they couldn't talk to each other about their work.

Elizebeth managed this better than William. Partly because what she was doing was a big "ought not," something a woman shouldn't do. Flying in the face of expectations was always something she relished. The risks only added to the excitement. Somehow she could leave it all behind at the office, come home, and eat dinner with her family as if she'd spent the day at a library rather than figuring out plots against America.

While listening in on Duquesne's ring, Elizebeth and her unit had also been tracking spies in South America. At first, the Nazis used codes similar to those the Prohibition rumrunners had used. These messages were easy to crack.

But then the Germans and their agents started relying on the Enigma machine.

In fact, she saw the Germans were using three different machines: one for diplomatic cables (nicknamed Blue), one for the Abwehr (the German Military Intelligence Service, nicknamed Green), and one for the SS (the Nazi paramilitary organization that was fanatically loyal to Adolf Hitler, nicknamed Red and the trickiest of the three).

Elizebeth and her team needed to crack all of them.

SPYING ON SPIES

The British desperately needed the United States as an ally, just as they had in the First World War. Secret agents were sent to convince the American government to spy on the Germans and Japanese, even if it wouldn't actively join the war. Two of these spies later became famous writers, one for children—Roald Dahl, of *Charlie and the Chocolate Factory* fame—and one for adults—Ian Fleming, creator of James Bond.

The British agents also talked directly with Elizebeth, aware of the important work she was doing for the Coast Guard. Colonel F. J. M. Stratton, an astrophysicist working in the British Army's Royal Corps of Signals, asked Elizebeth personally if they could share intelligence. Between England and the US Coast Guard, they could intercept radio messages all over the world. Stratton treated her with respect, and Elizebeth liked him right away. He looked, she said, like Santa Claus and was equally jolly. But he was also smart and focused, determined to defeat the Germans.

The decoding unit Elizebeth had set up in the Coast Guard focused with renewed intensity, worried about what the Nazis could do. Henry Morgenthau Jr., the secretary of the Treasury, realized from looking at the decryptions that "someone inside the office of the President of Brazil is in the employ of the Nazis. I am informed that a particularly complicated code was used for sending this series of messages." This was a real and pressing danger.

The goal was to avoid a Nazi takeover of South America. President Roosevelt warned of the risks in his fireside chat to the American people on December 29, 1940: "Any South American country, in Nazi hands, would constitute a jumping-off place for German attack on any one of the other republics in the hemisphere." Meaning the United States.

Elizebeth's unit intercepted more than 10,000 messages from 65 different German circuits (radio stations regularly communicating with each other). Of these, her team cracked more than 8,500, an impressively high success rate. All this without the help of computers. Elizebeth, like William, like everyone in her unit, used paper, pencil, and brainpower. Nothing more.

It's widely known that Alan Turing in Britain cracked Enigma, using a proto-computer and a staff of 10,000 (75 percent of whom were women). The team was housed outside of London in Bletchley Park, a big campus where

SPYING ON SPIES

code-breakers lived and worked together. The movie *The Imitation Game* has made their work famous. Elizebeth remains forgotten, though she came up with the first Enigma wiring solution in the United States at about the same time as Turing's group, without anywhere near the staff and with zero computing power. How did she do it?

William had shown her the way. At the end of World War I, he had seen a new machine developed by Edward Hebern to encrypt documents. The machine looked like a typewriter but used rotors to change the letter typed into a completely random one. William thought Hebern's machine wasn't secure enough. He could crack it easily. Having looked carefully at it, however, he was prepared for the later complexity of the Enigma machine, which used three rotors and was much more sophisticated than Hebern's device with its single rotor. The two machines followed the same principle, however. What William and Elizebeth both saw was that if a cryptanalyst had enough messages to compare, they could discover patterns, and those patterns would reveal possible settings for the rotors.

Just as Elizebeth had seen in the Chinese business code, certain phrases were sure to appear in these Nazi messages—"Heil Hitler," for example, would be at the end of every letter. Dates and times would also be regular features. This predictability gave code-breakers a place to start.

Realizing how to crack machines like Enigma led William to develop his own machine. With the help of one of his fellow code-breakers, Frank Rowlett, the two invented SIGABA, the highest-security device used by the United States during World War II. SIGABA was a machine like Enigma. Only it was never cracked by the Germans, Japanese, or Italians, the three countries fighting together as the Axis powers.

Enigma, on the other hand, was cracked by both the Americans and the British. The Nazis, superior though they saw themselves, didn't have anyone like Elizebeth and William working on their side.

SIXTEEN

THE SOUTH AMERICAN ENIGMA

In 1941, Elizebeth started tracking a powerful, effective Nazi spy. His code name was "Sargo." Elizebeth's team would discover that this man with forty-seven aliases and several false passports was really Johannes Siegfried Becker, part of an elite SS unit.

Sargo seemed to be all over South America. Elizebeth heard him giving instructions, asking questions, recruiting spies, setting up radio stations. He controlled hundreds of Nazi agents throughout several countries. He used all three different codes, depending on which agency he was working with: the SS, the Abwehr, or the German Embassy.

Another code name caught Elizebeth's attention. This was "Luna," who seemed to be in charge of setting up radio stations and sending messages for different Nazi agencies. He warned fellow spies never to repeat themselves, to vary the times when they radioed messages, to follow the correct protocol using the Enigma machines. Above all, never be predictable.

Luna turned out to be Wolf Franczok, an SS radio engineer.

The last code name that appeared often was "Alfredo." As a German businessman married to a Brazilian woman, Alfredo—or really Albrecht Engels—was perfectly positioned to act as an agent for the Abwehr. The only thing Elizebeth's team knew about him at first was that he had a broad reach and seemed to be everywhere.

SPYING ON SPIES

Elizebeth heard lots of enemy chatter about American politics, factory capabilities, positions of ships in the seas, plus ideas of how to keep America isolated and out of the war. One decrypted message read: "Try with all means to find out the state of USA research in the field of propulsion weapons as well as projectiles." This led Elizebeth's team to discover and follow agents working within America.

Elizebeth's unit listened carefully to any messages from the German U-boats, which presented a serious threat to the Allies. These Nazi submarines lurked off the British coasts, sinking ships bringing supplies and troops, as well as those leaving England. Boats full of refugees, even children, were targeted. When Allied ships were in danger of being sunk by German U-boats, the decoded secret messages helped save lives, warning ships where the attackers lurked. Luna blamed sloppy radio operators repeating themselves. He never thought Enigma had been cracked. He thought that was impossible!

To President Roosevelt, it looked harder and harder to avoid the war engulfing so many allies. Germany had invaded Poland, France, Belgium, the Netherlands, and Denmark. In July 1941, Roosevelt tasked his son, James, and William "Wild Bill" Donovan, a brash former Army colonel, with creating the Office of the Coordinator of Information. They were to take over some of the work of the Signal Corps and develop new systems for spying on enemies and communicating secretly with America's allies and agents. Both men had heard of Elizebeth. They knew how good she was at her job. Donovan declared an "urgent need for her services pending the establishment of our permanent code section."

Elizebeth, along with her five-person unit, was transferred from the Coast Guard to the new Office of the Coordinator of Information. Although as a woman she could hold no military rank and was a civilian, she was so valued that the military made an exception to put her in this high-level position.

Elizebeth's new job was to create codes to communicate with US agents in the field, as well as to continue listening to what enemy spies were saying. Cryptography was still only a tiny part of the US government. Only fifty people worked in the new discipline for the Army, the Navy, and the State Department combined! Contrast that to today, when roughly 21,000 people work for the CIA and as many as 55,000 for the NSA (National Security Agency)—not to mention the dozens of other agencies working on intelligence for each branch of the military. In only a month, Elizebeth set up an entire cryptographic system and devices to use for enciphering so that the United States could safely send its own secret messages. She didn't know it, but once again her work paralleled William's. The military branches that didn't have the use of William's SIGABA machines relied on Elizebeth's methods. Between the two of them, the military was well protected. Both created methods for analyzing codes and ciphers. Both created systems for sending secure communications.

Elizebeth did this with a much smaller team than William. But what she really minded was how Donovan barked orders as if she were a servant. In her small unit, she was used to having men listen to her. Even worse, she considered Donovan careless with security, arrogant, and sloppy, like Hoover at the FBI. She was worried enough to send James Roosevelt a list of recommendations for how to run an efficient and leakproof organization. Roosevelt respected her enough to implement them, though Donovan didn't always follow her guidance.

Then, on December 7, 1941, Pearl Harbor in Hawaii was attacked by a massive bombardment. More than 350 Japanese planes fired on American battleships and aircraft. The damage to the Pacific Fleet was horrifying. Every single battleship was damaged, twenty-one ships sunk, two hundred planes destroyed, and more than two thousand men killed. William took the attack personally—after all, he'd broken Purple. The Americans should have known of the coming attack. The Army did know that a major assault was planned for that day, but they said the target was unclear. Intelligence thought it would be Manila, in the Philippines.

William agonized over the catastrophe, sobbing, "But they knew, they knew." And that was how Elizebeth figured out that her husband had cracked Purple. All she could do now was comfort him. For years afterward, William tried to understand what had happened. One problem was that messages weren't passed quickly enough to where they needed to go. Pearl Harbor didn't have its own Purple machine to use for decrypting, so the military there had to wait for Magic decrypts to arrive by telegram. And there was the classic cryptanalytical dilemma—if the fleet had been protected, the Japanese would know their code had been broken. Do you take risks to keep a secret that may save hundreds of thousands of future lives? It was a difficult choice to make and not one for the decoders themselves to decide. William called these unsolvable problems "cryptologic schizophrenia . . . What to do?" As a decoder, his job was to pass on the decrypted messages. The military brass decided how to act on the information.

Some historians have speculated that the Army knew about the planned attack and allowed it to happen. That way, the American public would finally support their country joining the war. After World War I, the country had become strongly isolationist, not wanting to be involved in any more overseas conflicts. Pearl Harbor changed that. An attack on American soil? That was grounds for war!

Recently declassified reports from the NSA reveal

that William's decryption tools had worked as they should have. Messages in late November 1941 warned of attacks on the United States, specifically on Hawaii. General Walter C. Short, based in Pearl Harbor, issued an alert for sabotage in response to the warning. This was "like saying he had a butterfly net ready for a tiger." More decrypted messages followed on December 6, all threatening attacks on Hawaii, the Philippines, and the West Coast. Still, Admiral Husband Kimmel, also stationed at Pearl Harbor, thought additional warnings would "only confuse" the commanders in the field. General George Marshall sent a warning to Hawaii anyway at noon on December 7 through the Signal Corps, asking it to be delivered by Army radio (which would have been quick, direct contact). Instead, for never-explained reasons, the message was sent by commercial telegram and wouldn't arrive for another eight hours. Too late. Elizebeth imagined the messenger hiding in a ditch as Japanese warplanes flew overhead. And that is precisely what happened.

An hour after the message should have arrived, the Japanese attacked Pearl Harbor, inflicting massive damage on the naval fleet there. The next day, America declared war on Japan. Germany declared war on the United States in response. The time of isolationism, of waiting and watching, was over.

Elizabeth's spy work mattered now more than ever. In some ways, her work was even more secret than William's because she was dealing with counterespionage—spying on spies.

SEVENTEEN

UNIT 387

Having finished the assignment of setting up coding protocols for the *Office of the Coordinator of Information* (a mouthful of a title), Elizebeth was eager to return to the *Coast Guard* under US Navy command. She wanted to get away from Donovan and return to her work monitoring Nazi agents. With America now officially at war, the task was more urgent than ever.

I'm tired of politics and red tape— there's too much work to be done!

She was assigned to the newly formed Unit 387 and given the mission to intercept and decode messages from the enemy in the Western Hemisphere. As part of the military, Unit 387 was a place where rank mattered. Elizebeth, as a woman and a civilian, would no longer be cryptanalyst-in-charge but a mere cryptanalyst.

Welcome to our unit!

Luckily, the officer in command had trained with William and had worked with Elizebeth before. Lt. Commander Jones knew her abilities.

SPYING ON SPIES

Now that war had been declared, the tone of the messages was darker. Sargo was pressuring the Argentine government to accept German aid. The Nazis offered to help Argentina take over the entire continent, just as they themselves were sweeping through all of Europe. But with America in the war, there were now major distractions. Brazil had declared loyalty to the United States. Sargo and his spies fought back by reporting the positions of Brazilian ships, passing on targets to German U-boats, which then torpedoed them. Brazil knew German spies were responsible, even if they couldn't prove it. They retaliated by sanctioning German businesses and freezing financial accounts.

Elizebeth decoded one spy's complaint that "measures against members of the Axis [Germany, Japan, and Italy] are assuming drastic form. Bank deposits already blocked. We are destroying all compromising documents, maintaining radio operation as long as possible. Heil Hitler." Still, the agents were allowed to operate freely by the Brazilian authorities. No arrests were made, and the radio stations kept sending coded messages.

One message revealed a plan to sink the troopship RMS *Queen Mary*, carrying more than 8,000 American soldiers. Hitler had offered one million Reichsmarks and the Iron Cross medal to the Nazi captain who could destroy the ship. Despite the risk that the Germans might realize their code had been cracked, Elizebeth told the head of the Navy to warn the captain of the *Queen Mary*, letting him know where the U-boats were hiding, something her decrypts had revealed. The troopship changed course, zigzagging through the ocean to avoid the U-boats' deadly torpedoes. The Nazis were disappointed but so confident in the Enigma machine, they thought they had lost the target through sheer bad luck.

Elizebeth kept watch as the Germans looked for information on American and British ships so they could sink them with their U-boats. Before her unit started decoding radio intercepts, the Allies had suffered huge losses, more than 1,000 ships sunk in 1942 with 5,000 lives lost, many more than at Pearl Harbor. The following year, with Elizebeth's help, fewer than two hundred ships were torpedoed.

On land, Sargo's agents were getting more and more

worried. Elizebeth's team heard about actual arrests now. In both Chile and Brazil, spies found their hiding places searched. They warned each other about police raids. And then there was radio silence as the police in both countries rounded up the Nazi agents. Ironically, this was bad news for Elizebeth's unit. They needed the spies left alone so they could listen to their plans, learn about the enemy's strengths and intentions.

The FBI didn't care about the work of Unit 387. Hoover was pressuring South American allies to crack down on German agents, to arrest them all. On March 10, 1942, police in Brazil caught Josef Starziczny (known to Elizebeth as "Lucas"), the Nazi agent who had blabbed the location of the *Queen Mary*. Though it was Elizebeth's team who had decrypted the messages and alerted the captain, the FBI took credit for saving the ship after the war ended. In fact, Hoover presented all of Unit 387's successes as his own. In an impressive public relations job, he showcased the FBI as much more effective and strategic than it actually was. To this day, the FBI doesn't acknowledge any of Elizebeth's work and still claims her unit's achievements as its own.

Elizebeth didn't care about the credit. She cared about having her spy networks silenced, leaving her team totally in the dark. Would the Nazi operatives know that Enigma had been cracked and devise an even more difficult cipher? Would Elizebeth's team have to start all over?

EIGHTEEN

AVOIDING THE FBI

In February 1942, the US Coast Guard and the US Navy decided not to send decrypted messages to the FBI anymore but only summaries of the information. The FBI had proven careless with the information it was given, leading to the German sinking of at least one allied ship.

British intelligence was also suspicious of the FBI and asked that any information about Enigma decryptions be kept from the sloppy agency. Elizebeth's unit's decoded messages were no longer passed on. By late 1943, Hoover realized his agency wasn't receiving the information he expected.

Hoover, for once, backed down.

SPYING ON SPIES

Elizebeth was respected enough to be included in a meeting in April 1942 coordinating cryptography between American, Canadian, and British agencies. The only woman in the room, Elizebeth was listed in the official notes as Mr. Friedman, with the s in Mrs. whited out. It had to have been a typo, after all!

The British attending the meeting wanted to invite Elizebeth to Bletchley Park to share thoughts on the Enigma systems, but Major G. G. Stevens in England believed that "it would be more suitable to send Lieutenant Commander Jones, the official head of the section." Elizebeth was clearly the better cryptographer, but she was a civilian and a woman. Elizebeth did go to Bletchley Park, however—with Lieutenant Commander Jones. An agreement for sharing decrypts and solutions was arranged, but the details of what was discussed still remain classified to this day. And Elizebeth never said a word about her time at Bletchley Park.

Though other agencies were helping Elizebeth's unit now, the FBI's carelessness continued to make their work much harder.

Hearing of Josef Starziczny's arrest, the Abwehr agent Albrecht Engels (code name Alfredo) managed to get a radio transmitter, Enigma code books, and nearly $90,000 in cash to fellow spies before his own arrest that spring, in 1942. He also warned Berlin of the collapse of Sargo's network. Almost ninety agents were held in prison by the Brazilian government. To Elizebeth, this was all bad news, the kind she'd been fearing. The entire continent would go silent, though the two biggest fish in the spy network—Sargo, the mastermind, and Luna, the radio operator—were still free. But there was worse news to come. Engels sent a warning to Berlin: "I fear that MEYER [another arrested spy] also given away the radio procedure therefore I shall lie low until further notice." In other words, the Germans now knew that Enigma was cracked. Engels thought the Brazilian police had confiscated code books and a machine from Starziczny and other agents. And he was right. But he didn't know that the Americans had solved Enigma long before that. Now, though, the Germans would change the protocol. Elizebeth's team would face a tough new code—or worse, silence.

Then Engels himself was arrested. But he remained an expert spy and managed to smuggle out one final message, using the wife of one of his colleagues. Berlin had to know that all Enigma codes had been broken. None of them were safe anymore. He warned, "Take all precautionary measures, above all, separate."

William, meanwhile, was still working on the Japanese Purple code at two American versions of England's Bletchley Park, both housed in old private school buildings in Washington, DC. One was at Arlington Hall, the other at the Naval Communications Annex. William had a much bigger staff now, though nowhere near the numbers at Bletchley. Many of these code-breakers, as in England, were women, either WACs (Women's Army Corps) or WAVES (Women Accepted for Volunteer Emergency Service, under the US Naval Reserve). There weren't enough men for the work with so many already serving in the military. William looked for recruits at women's colleges where students were trained in secret cryptology classes using the methods written up by Elizebeth and William. His marriage to Elizebeth had taught William never to underestimate women's skills or consider them lesser talent. He knew how smart, focused, and determined women could be.

As the arrests of Nazi agents continued in Brazil, Elizebeth's Coast Guard team, Unit 387, was moved to the

Naval Annex where William was working. They weren't in the same room or on the same team, but at least they shared a break room and cafeteria. And a more official presence. Now Elizebeth had the occasional use of rooms filled with IBM punch card machines. Early computing had come to decrypting. These machines weren't as big or as sophisticated as the "bombe" developed by Turing for Bletchley Park in Britain. But they helped run through ciphers quickly once the correct settings and decryption tools had been found by hand.

Elizebeth, however, still relied on pencil, paper, and brain power. Her team's allotted time to use the machines was too sporadic to mean much. The machines were mostly reserved for other intelligence units. Elizebeth had to depend on her mental faculties, as she always had. She would need to be at her sharpest, because Engels's warning meant that the Nazis had changed encryption tactics. There were still messages to be cracked, with new radio stations appearing all over South America. But Unit 387 and the British were both back to square one. And both were furious with the FBI for pressing for the spies' arrests and for tipping off the Germans to the Allies' ability to understand their codes.

Elizebeth didn't care about getting credit or accolades. She cared about getting the job done. She had lost faith in the FBI after the Duquesne case. Hoover was too sloppy and impatient. He chose quick results over long-term gains every time. And he hadn't learned from his mistakes, making things more difficult for everyone. Most of all, he didn't value spy-craft, didn't understand the hard work of the code-breakers. Thanks to him, Elizebeth and her team now faced new German codes and ciphers that were more sophisticated and much trickier to solve. As soon as Elizebeth cracked one code, another would appear. And the Nazis had spies everywhere—the Coast Guard tracked messages from Portugal, Morocco, West Africa, Iran, Crimea, Spain, France, Mozambique, Chile, Libya, Brazil, and Argentina. How could Elizebeth solve them all?

NINETEEN
CRACKING ENIGMA

Through intense focus, by the winter of 1942, Elizabeth's team was back on track, listening to intercepts. They'd broken every code except one. It looked like a new Enigma machine, more complicated than the others.

Elizebeth called it Circuit 3-N (later called Red) since the messages came over that circuit, between South America and Europe, probably between Buenos Aires and Berlin. The stronger coding meant the messages were more important, from the highest levels. Elizebeth guessed they were from the SS and contained essential information.

This was a problem she had to solve.

Argentina was a natural focus for the Nazis since the government favored Germany over the United States, unlike Brazil, which was strongly pro-America. Chile wavered between the two, keeping ties open with Germany until early 1943. The Nazi spy Luna set up a new radio station in Buenos Aires, waiting for his contact Sargo to arrive with a newly smuggled Enigma machine. By January 1943, both Luna and Sargo were ready to send and receive coded messages.

The three different German agencies still needed to communicate between spies in Argentina and Berlin. The German Embassy, the Abwehr, and the SS each asked Luna to build a separate radio station, as they had in Brazil before the crackdown. That was too difficult now. Instead, Luna set up one radio operation with a single Enigma machine but told each agency it was theirs alone to use with their specific settings. He gave each a different time for sending messages so none would know about the other. As before, Red was the SS, with Becker sending messages. Green was the Abwehr, with Hans Harnisch in charge of signals. Blue was the German Embassy. The three agencies often undercut one another, each fighting for power. If there were leaks, it was easy to blame someone in a competing intelligence office.

Together Sargo and Luna recruited new spies, mostly in Argentina, where they seemed to be headquartered, to make up for all the arrests in Brazil. They ended up with forty-two agents, training them to send messages at different times of day and to include "garbage" messages, utter nonsense to throw off anyone who might be listening. Luna emphasized the protocol to never, never repeat a message. He was still sure that was how any ciphers had been cracked—through German sloppiness, not Allied cleverness. With the new Enigma machine, Luna expected to be overheard but not understood.

Elizebeth quickly amassed a pile of twenty-eight Enigma messages. Now maybe she had enough to find a way in. She started by counting letter frequency, just as she had always done, noticing patterns. Certain letter combinations could be guessed at. For instance, seeing the letters *CQA* in an English message over and over again could be interpreted as *THE*, the most common three-letter word. Elizebeth had solved an earlier Enigma in 1940, and Turing had shared Bletchley Park's solution to the European Enigma in December

1942. But this South American system was completely different.

Taking the piles of messages and looking for patterns, Elizebeth's team cracked the Green circuit (the Abwehr) first.

The messages revealed that something big was being planned from Argentina, but amid all the chatter, it was hard to tease out precise information. Some messages were trivial distractions, sending love to family members back home or asking about a relative's health. Others were more significant and followed expected patterns, asking about American military and factory capabilities. But the contacts made by Sargo and Luna felt more sinister. They were building a secret army of Nazi supporters with deep ties to the Argentine government. Elizebeth feared they were stoking revolutions to spread across South America.

On June 4, 1943, the generals in Argentina staged a coup. They threw out the elected president and installed Pedro Pablo Ramirez, a puppet controlled by the military. Colonel Juan Perón was part of the coup and had close Nazi ties. Elizebeth's group found evidence that Perón and later his wife, Eva, were Nazi agents. Perón met with the Abwehr to plan how Argentina could create instability in neighboring countries and ultimately rule all of South America just as Germany would rule all of Europe. The plan was for Ecuador to fall first, followed by Chile, Bolivia, Paraguay, then Brazil. All the countries would become puppet states controlled by Argentina and Germany. The next step would be North America. In late August, Elizebeth cracked the message that spelled out the plan:

"Final objective is said to be formation of a block of South American countries" under Argentine and German rule.

In December 1943, Elizebeth's unit decrypted messages about planned German-backed revolutions in Bolivia and Chile. Thanks to the early warning, both coup attempts failed. Her group also had evidence about planned attacks in the Caribbean and helped thwart a planned invasion of the island of Martinique. There were so many plots, it was hard to keep them all straight.

The news grew bleaker as Elizebeth's unit traced a secret weapons deal for Germany to get guns and bombs to Argentina. Perón needed the weapons to fight Brazil, but it would be difficult to get them, since the Nazis, battling both the Russians and the Americans, needed firepower themselves. Osmar Hellmuth, the Argentine envoy, was directed to go to Germany and beg for the weapons in person. He was told to make an impassioned plea for how all of South America could work for Germany and directly threaten the United States. Sending the weapons would be an important investment in Germany's future world domination!

Hellmuth was a low-ranking naval officer and seemed the perfect choice for such a delicate mission. He wasn't important enough to attract any attention. And he had an embassy position, which made him untouchable. Diplomatic immunity would protect him from any possible arrest since diplomats all over the world were shielded from other countries' laws.

Elizebeth listened to the plans, waiting for the right moment to act. The Coast Guard and the Navy knew what was at stake. They didn't want to rush in too quickly, as the FBI had. They waited. And listened some more.

TWENTY

WHEN TO ACT ON INTELLIGENCE

October 2, 1943. Hellmuth set sail for Germany with a shopping list of weapons and a strategy for how to sell the Nazis on the important role Argentina could play in the Reich's world domination.

With Argentina sparking wars throughout South America, the United States would have to leave Germany alone. Instead, the Americans would need to turn all their attention to their nearby southern neighbor.

If they didn't, the newly powerful Argentina would invade Central America, then Mexico, then the United States itself. It would be glorious.

While waiting for Hellmuth to cross the Atlantic, Elizebeth's team listened as the network prepared to spark coups throughout South America. Once the new governments were in place, they would attack the United States, starting with the Navy. A Chilean gunnery sergeant who had taken a training course with the US Navy provided essential help with his insider knowledge. This type of training wasn't unusual, since Chile was considered an ally, not an enemy. The sergeant, however, was definitely an enemy. Elizebeth listened as he passed on valuable details about weaknesses and system operations. Everything was in place. The only thing missing was the weaponry to make it all happen.

The Allies could not allow Hellmuth to reach Germany. The Coast Guard had shared the unit's intercepts with the British. While Hellmuth's ship was docked in Trinidad, a British special forces unit grabbed him in the middle of the night in a secret operation. He wasn't seen as a major figure, so he had no special protection. Hellmuth himself was too meek to put up any kind of fight. The British soldiers got him off the ship without any of the crew noticing. It was all over quickly and quietly without anybody knowing that a diplomat had been taken prisoner.

When the ship arrived in Germany and nothing was heard from Hellmuth, Argentina was immediately suspicious. Had the Allies found out about Hellmuth's mission somehow? The ambassador asked the British government if they knew where their diplomat was. Naturally, the English had no idea.

Meanwhile Hellmuth was interrogated. The letter of instructions and the detailed shopping list were found, proving him to be a Nazi spy, not a diplomat with immunity from the law. That was enough to get him talking. Hellmuth wasn't a trained spy. He quickly told the British everything he knew—that the new Argentine government was working closely with the Nazis, that coups were planned throughout South America, that a Chilean sergeant had brought back information about American naval systems. All of this would allow the Nazification of South America. He even named the masterminds—Luna and Sargo.

Back in Argentina, the Nazis had no idea Hellmuth had been captured. Their coup plans still looked strong. On December 20, 1943, the first of the series of government ousters succeeded. Bolivia's government was thrown out, replaced with a new pro-Nazi regime. The coup attempt in Chile was stopped, however, thanks to Elizebeth alerting the right people in time.

The Red Enigma code, the SS one, still hadn't been broken, though Elizebeth's team felt closer than ever. More messages piled in, offering more chances to compare patterns and frequencies. The question was when they would have enough for a breakthrough.

The British weren't worried that the Nazis would suspect Enigma messages had been cracked. The information they had obviously came from a human source—Hellmuth—not radio messages. They weren't worried about explaining how Hellmuth had ended up in British control, either. After all, Trinidad was a British colony. Hellmuth could have wandered around drunk in port and been picked up by police unaware of his diplomatic status. Once he was arrested and the incriminating documents found, any diplomatic protection vanished.

Armed with this information, the Allies confronted Argentina about their close ties to the Nazis. They forced the Argentine government to denounce any connections to the Nazi regime or face sharp repercussions. On January 26, 1944, the Argentine government broke all official connections with Germany and Japan.

The next month, Elizebeth did the impossible—it had taken a year and a half, but she cracked Red. She and her team finally had amassed enough messages to spot the repeated patterns of key words. Quickly, her unit sent a secret cable to the British at Bletchley Park, letting them know of their success, promising that details for how to crack it would follow. Bletchley replied, "details not required." They had each solved Red at the same time, paper and pencil proving equal to computing power.

TWENTY-ONE

LISTENING TO THE GESTAPO

The Nazis in Argentina believed that Hellmuth was the leak, nothing else. They considered their encryption secure.

Losing Hellmuth and the hope for German weapons made things more difficult, but the spies weren't finished with their plots. Berlin wasn't done with South America, either. It was too centrally positioned to abandon. As the war in Europe faltered for Germany, South America was more important than ever. Some Nazis hoped that in a worst-case scenario, the Reich could be reborn there.

SPYING ON SPIES

Elizebeth's unit could now decode messages from the Gestapo to agents in South America. One warned: "There is a leak in your courier organization." Like Luna, the agent assumed that the Allies were getting information about the Nazi plans from people, not from listening in on the latest Enigma. The Gestapo agent went on to assure his spies that the rift between the Argentine government and Germany was just a show to fool the Americans. "Operation concerning unrest and South America must now even more go on in full revolutions." The plan to set up puppet governments throughout the continent would continue.

The next messages from the Gestapo to Sargo asked about chemical weapons in the United States, about the possibility of blowing up warehouses where the dangerous chemicals were stored, creating powerful dirty bombs. Not only would that sabotage production, but the chemicals would also kill many Americans. The chaos and panic would be huge! Elizebeth's team paid close attention, holding their breath that they would learn nothing so dangerous that they would have to act, which would reveal that the Allies had cracked the code. How close were the Nazis to making their evil plan work?

Were these suggestions or real plans? If Unit 387 had to save lives, they would, even if it meant the Germans turning to a new, more complicated Enigma machine.

The newspapers, meanwhile, featured bold, splashy headlines about the "Hellmuth Affair." The vast entrenched network of Nazis throughout South America was big, scary news. The coups in Argentina and Bolivia were seen as proof of Nazi control of local governments. Hoover was furious that the FBI had been kept in the dark about what was happening, especially once he learned that everyone else had known. He insisted that his agency had to be in South America, arresting the Nazi agents and putting pressure on Argentina to prove the country wasn't taking orders from Germany anymore.

The FBI scoured South America for spies. The Argentine government was forced to hand over any information they had. Hoover offered them a trade—he would sell a story about Argentina breaking its connections to evil Nazis, putting the government in a good light, if they would give him the two ringleaders, Sargo and Luna. Argentina, which still didn't have any of the hoped-for German weapons, had no choice but to agree. At least in theory.

SPYING ON SPIES

Nazi agents and radio stations were swept up, one by one, though somehow Sargo and Luna always managed to escape. Elizebeth and Unit 387 were in the dark once again. But now there was nothing to listen for. The spy ring had been decisively broken, even if the two masterminds behind it hadn't been caught.

After the war, the Navy summarized the success of Elizebeth's unit: "The ability to read the enemy's messages shortened the war by perhaps as much as two years and saved tens of thousands of Allied lives."

TWENTY-TWO

THE DOLL LADY

A new spy case blared in the headlines now, this one happening right in the United States.

Censors noticed the first suspicious letter and brought it to the FBI in February 1942. The letter was signed by a woman in Portland, Oregon, and mailed to Argentina.

Four more letters followed, all sent to Buenos Aires but coming from different people. One, supposedly from a Colorado woman, was postmarked Oakland, California, and mentioned seven small dolls making up a family.

When the FBI connected the "seven dolls" to seven warships sent to San Francisco Bay for repairs around the same time the letter was sent, their suspicions sharpened.

None of the supposed senders admitted to writing the letters. The signatures were forgeries.

The supposed writers all turned out to have connections with Dickinson. The FBI focused all its attention on the fifty-year-old widow.

The FBI had its own cryptography unit, people Elizebeth herself had trained. That team could see the letters were in some kind of code, but just like in the Duquesne case, they couldn't crack it. After months of getting nowhere, Hoover was forced once again to turn to Elizebeth.

The first letter was dated January 27, 1942, and read (typographical errors in original):

My Most Gracious Friend,

Please forgive my delay in writing to thank you for your kindness in sending my family the beautiful Christmas gifts. The girls were especially pleased.

I have been so very busy these days, this is the first time I have been over to Seattle for weeks. I came over today to meet my son who is here from Portland on business and to get my little granddaughters doll repaired. I must tell you this amusing story, the wife of an important business associate gave her an old German bisque Doll dressed in a Hulu Grass skirt. It is a cheap horrid thing I do Not like it and wish we did not have to have it about. Well I broke this awful doll last month now the person who gave the doll is coming to visit us very soon. I walked all over Seattle to get someone to repair it, no one at home could or would try the task. Now I expect all the damages to be repaired by the first week in February. In the meanwhile I hope and pray the Important gentlemen's wife will not come to visit us untill after that date.

SPYING ON SPIES

I do hope you can read my typing. I am trying to learn to type so I can be able to type records for the Red Cross.

Please accept love and rememberances sent to you form Elizebeth.

Sincerely

Maud Bowman

For Elizebeth, this was an easy task—the letter wasn't encrypted but in "open code," that is, words substituted for different meanings in a way that wasn't too complicated to decipher. She recognized the code as a clumsy one, divided into three basic parts. The first part was what she called "alibi language," words meant to cover up real identities. So the actual sender wasn't Maud Bowman, nor was the intended recipient really Señora Inez, as was typed on the envelope. As Elizebeth explained, "Common practice among undercover agents is to change the feminine to masculine and vice versa, and I have a more or less distinct feeling that 'Señora Inez' is really meant to be Mr. 'Martinez.'"

The next part was "authenticating signals." These were prearranged words meant to prove you were the right sender, someone the recipient could trust. In this case, Elizebeth saw the sentences about typing and greetings from a specific name as serving that purpose.

The most important part was "actual code language," that is, the important information being given. In this case, Elizebeth took the coded words to refer to Pearl Harbor and certain battleships damaged in the attack: "my family" = Japanese fleet or group of agents; "Christmas gifts" = Pearl Harbor attack; "girls" = Japanese naval officers or agents; the visit of the "Important gentlemen's wife" = invitation to attack/bomb Pearl Harbor. Put together, Elizebeth translated the letter as follows:

This is somewhat belated rejoicing over the victory at Pearl Harbor. The Japanese Navy is to be much congratulated for their good work. We, their friends here, are elated over it. (Please recognize your authorized correspondent. I am in Seattle and have the following to report).

There is a battleship here, damaged at Pearl Harbor, being repaired. It is one of the older battleships; but it is considered of sufficient value to be worthy of repair. It is expected the repairs will be completed by the first week in February. I wish that the Japanese could make a visit to the Navy Yard here and destroy it completely before that time.

(I hope the reference to my poor typing, like the paragraph above referring to family, will convince you that I am your authorized correspondent for this type of information.)

(Another signal of authentication is personal greetings from "Elizabeth.")

Elizebeth also discovered that the letters, sent to Buenos Aires, were all deliberately misaddressed so that the censor there, a friend of the Axis, would get the information into the right Japanese and Nazi hands.

The FBI found a lot of corroborating evidence. Velvalee, the Doll Lady, was a member of a Japanese-American society and had social connections with a Japanese consular official. More than that, right after Pearl Harbor, she had traveled with her husband to the West Coast, where she could gain the information included in the letters. Her travels suspiciously co-incided with certain battleships being repaired in Seattle, Oakland, and San Francisco. Even more incriminating, the typewriters used for the letters matched those at the hotels where the couple had stayed. Most suspicious of all, when the FBI searched her safe deposit box, it found wads of cash, nearly $13,000, traceable to a Japanese bank. This was a lot of evidence, but it could all be considered circumstantial. What the FBI lacked was a way to connect the cash to the Japanese agent who had paid Velvalee. Without clear proof of a Japanese contact, the letters remained the strongest basis for any legal case.

For Elizebeth, this was an easy job. She quickly decoded the letters. Some struck her as especially obvious, such as one mentioning "Mr. Shaw," a reference to the destroyer, USS *Shaw*. Another letter misspelled the Kentucky city as "Louville" to mean the battleship, USS *Louisville*. One letter used "rock garden" to refer to ammunition factories. Another signaled that repaired ships were back out to sea by saying something was "no longer in shops."

Elizebeth would have considered the writer a complete amateur, but she also saw suggestions that Velvalee had accomplices, sources for some information not personally gathered, which she gave to her American contact rather than sending to Argentina. The idea of a spy ring on American soil alarmed the FBI, and it quickly arrested Velvalee.

A slight, older woman, Velvalee looked completely innocent, but she was the first woman accused as a spy on American soil since the start of World War II. The FBI thought she would quickly confess, given the searing evidence of the letters. She didn't.

Velvalee did admit to typing the letters but insisted her husband had told her what to write. As for the money in the safe deposit box, it had been put there by her husband, as well. Her husband was the real spy. At the most, Velvalee might have broken a few censorship rules, nothing more.

Conveniently for her, the spy husband had died the previous year from a heart condition. The FBI didn't believe he was the real spy, but the evidence for blaming Velvalee by herself now looked more tenuous. Mr. Dickinson hadn't had any connections to Japanese officials. He hadn't known the Japanese naval attaché as his wife did. And his doctor testified that at the time of the alleged payment, Mr. Dickinson was both physically and mentally impaired. But a jury could well sympathize with a grieving widow. After all, who was more likely to be a spy, a man or a woman?

The FBI felt it had no choice. The agency offered to drop the espionage charge if Velvalee would plead guilty to the censorship violation. Since she'd already admitted that, it was an easy agreement for Velvalee to make. She felt safe with her dead husband now labeled the real spy.

To her shock, the plea didn't help Velvalee the way she had expected. The judge sentenced her to the maximum for the censorship violation, ten years in prison and a fine of $10,000. He justified his decision by saying, "The indictment to which you have pleaded guilty is a serious matter; it borders close to treason. You were fortunate that the Government did not have you tried on espionage charges."

An unknown source (perhaps her Japanese contact) paid the fine for her, but the Doll Lady served seven years before she was released. Once again, the case made big headlines for the FBI. As always, Elizebeth was relieved to stay well out of the media glare.

The FBI took full credit for the arrest then and still does today. There is no mention of Elizebeth's role other than a vague reference to "FBI cryptographers."

SPYING ON SPIES

Elizebeth wasn't fond of Hoover's bluster, but this was actually how she preferred to work, behind the scenes. The days of her testifying in court and dealing with newspaper reporters were long over. Spies acted in secret, and the people who listened in on them needed to do the same. For Elizebeth, that was the essence of good spy-craft.

TWENTY-THREE

THE LAST SPIES

Elizebeth's Christmas letter that year didn't mention the Doll Lady. Instead, she boasted about her kids. And for once, she didn't write in code.

John excelled at his prep school—he was president of the Senior Club and managed the football team.

Barbara was working at the US Office of Censorship in Panama, following in her parents' footsteps in government work.

With the Doll Lady case over, Elizebeth turned her attention once again to tracking Nazi spies in South America. On August 18, 1944, the Argentine Federal Police finally caught Luna along with forty other radio agents and spies. They offered their arrests as proof of Argentina's break with Germany, at least on the surface, though Luna wasn't handed over to the FBI, as had been promised.

Juan Perón, the popular army general and vice president of the country's military dictatorship, went to the prison where the spies were held to order the prison administration that any "mention of contact with any political or military personalities or their foreign colleagues must be suppressed." Luna told the FBI later that the Argentinian authorities didn't want to punish him. They just wanted to cover up their own ties to the Nazis.

There were no more spy networks in South America, no more radio stations, though Sargo still hadn't been caught. Had he made his way back to Berlin somehow? Or was Perón shielding him, hiding him along with his own complicity with the Germans?

Elizebeth and Unit 387 had cracked forty-eight different radio circuits, three Enigma machines, and more than four thousand encrypted messages. And with this crushing defeat, the Nazis lost their hopes that a Fourth Reich would be born in South America from the ashes of the Third. As usual, Hoover took full credit for this impressive feat in a story in the *American Magazine*, "How the Nazi Spy Invasion Was Smashed."

The war was winding down. On April 19, 1945, Sargo, the last Nazi spy in Argentina, the brains behind it all, was finally arrested by the Argentine police. He blabbed right away, making it clear that he could implicate Perón directly. Perón was positioning himself to run for president and didn't want ugly rumors—or worse, the truth—to spread about his close connections to the Nazis. So Perón silenced Sargo by giving him cushy quarters in prison, complete with champagne and fine dining. As soon as he won the presidential election in June, Perón had Sargo released. Again, the promise to the FBI to arrest all Nazi agents had been forgotten.

Sargo stayed in the country, having been promised that he would be well taken care of. He passed on the favor, smoothing the way to bring in and settle Nazi war criminals. Luna, who had also been quickly released, went back to Germany. Neither of the two major masterminds of the South American spy network faced any punishment for their work, not in Argentina, America, or Germany.

On April 30, shortly after Sargo's arrest, Hitler killed himself in his underground bunker, leaving Germany to surrender. Japan surrendered a few months later, in August 1945.

The last part of Elizebeth's work in South America was presenting all the information she had gathered on Juan Perón and his work as a Nazi agent for years. But he wasn't arrested by the FBI. Hoover considered him too powerful, too influential with the Argentine Army. The former US ambassador to Argentina thought something should be done, anyway. In February 1946, he used Elizebeth's information to publish a report on Perón's Nazi ties. It came to be known as the notorious "Blue Book." It traced clear connections to the Nazi spy ring that had plotted coups throughout Latin America. It described how Perón had worked to bring into power fascist governments sympathetic to the Germans.

Perón responded by accusing the former ambassador himself of being part of the circle of spies. Popular with the people, Perón used his lying counterattack to convince the voters, and he served three terms as president until he was deposed in a coup. Under Perón, Argentina was a fascist haven for Nazis. They were offered complete protection by the president. Adolf Eichmann and Josef Mengele were among the high-level Nazi war criminals who made comfortable homes in Perón's Argentina.

Elizebeth had done what she could, but code-breakers could only reach so far. At least she had saved American lives. Punishing Nazis wasn't her job. Finding them was.

TWENTY-FOUR

A LIBRARY OF CODES

After years of tense listening and decoding, the work of Unit 387 was over. Elizebeth stayed at the office now not to crack codes but to archive them. She organized files for every single cipher her team had solved.

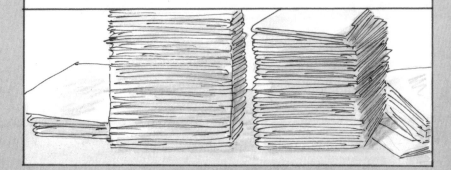

Then she went to the *Coast Guard* to archive those codes and ciphers. Once this library of secrets was finished, she recommended that her unit be closed, kicking herself out of a job.

Before she left, she had to sign a secrecy oath.

She couldn't ever tell anyone about her work during World War II. On September 12, 1946, she was sent home, a regular civilian after decades working on the most secret of secrets. She had walked in the door as a master of spies.

She walked out the door as an ordinary middle-aged woman whose mind held extraordinary secrets.

SPYING ON SPIES

Elizebeth kept her oath. Many years later, when she gave interviews, she spoke freely about her work during World War I and Prohibition, but she never said a word about what she did during World War II. We only know about her achievements now because the National Security Agency (NSA) has recently declassified many documents linked to her work. But not everything is open to the public. There are more secrets about Elizebeth waiting for the future to uncover.

With free time ahead of her after many decades of intense work, Elizebeth went to visit Barbara at Radcliffe College and then John at the US Army Air Corps, which he had joined directly from boarding school. And she hoped to work once more on projects with her husband.

William also had to swear an oath of secrecy, but he wasn't done with military service yet. He was sent to Germany to sweep up any intelligence left behind by the Nazis. He collected machines, coding, and cryptography and found several ingenious inventions. One encrypted the human voice the same way Enigma encrypted texts. Another scrambled speech so it was incomprehensible. Yet another was a kind of "acoustic torpedo," shooting bullets of sound at U-boats to cloak them from radar.

These inventions all intrigued William, but the most satisfying discovery was that the Germans had never broken SIGABA, the cipher machine he'd invented with Frank Rowlett. Every German and Japanese Enigma machine had been cracked by William's team, by Elizebeth's, and by Bletchley Park.

Elizebeth had one last cryptography project. The International Monetary Fund hired her to set up a secure communications system. This was as much about secret information as about safeguarding money, where it was, and how it was being moved. After creating and managing the secure system, Elizebeth retired, in 1947. She was done working for others, but she wasn't done with codes.

Nor was William. The couple wrote a last book together, and not on military codes at all. This new book was all about how Francis Bacon did *not* write Shakespeare's plays, despite the popular theory that he had. The couple hearkened back to their early days at Riverbank and wrote *Ciphers Examined*, the story of how people see what they want to see when what really matters is following the truth. William had stayed in touch with Fabyan until his death in 1936. He remained grateful for the chance the millionaire had given him, the profession

Fabyan had created for him. Elizebeth was less generous in her feelings toward their old patron. But she was nostalgic for their time at Riverbank and the world that had opened up for her there.

It seemed fitting for them to return to their start in code-breaking, to emphasize that the truth mattered more than indulging preconceptions. And to go back to language, the thing that had fascinated them both from the beginning. That is what they had done their entire lives, looked for the truth—in literary texts, in World War I radio intercepts, in criminal codes, and in World War II by spying on spies. Through all the tangled information they had sorted through, they kept their focus on impartial readings, determined to avoid seeing what they wanted to see rather than what was really there. Knowledge is power, the kind of power that mattered most to them.

The only code the two master code-breakers couldn't crack wasn't a complicated machine at all but a Renaissance manuscript. The Voynich manuscript is a handwritten illustrated book written in a strange cipher. The parchment it's written on dates from the early 1400s and was probably made in Italy. Some pages are missing, but there are still 240 left, enough for any pattern to be revealed. The text seems to be written from left to right and includes art. Many pages have illustrations or diagrams of people, animals, plants, and astronomical charts. William tried for years to solve the code, as have many others. Elizebeth helped for a while but left the project to William. To this day, it remains a mystery. You can see the book at the Yale University Beinecke Rare Book and Manuscript Library and try for yourself to figure it out. William could crack the complicated machine-derived Purple but was defeated by an early Renaissance book. Sometimes the pen truly is mightier than the machine, a result that Elizebeth would heartily approve.

TWENTY-FIVE

ONE FINAL CODE

William died in 1969. On his tombstone, Elizebeth had engraved a final code: "Knowledge Is Power."

How is that a code? She used the system that Bacon supposedly had used to send the secret messages in Shakespeare's plays, by mixing letter forms. That is, some letters had serifs (extra lines, like this: **A B C**) and some didn't (plain letters, like this: A B C).

KNOWLEDGE IS POWER

Look carefully at KNOWLEDGE IS POWER and you can see which letters have the extra little lines we call serifs. It's easier to see if we capitalize the serif letters and put the sans serif letters in lower case. Then you get: KnOwl edGeI spOwE r. We're splitting up the words into groups of five since that's how the Baconian cipher worked. Each serif letter is "b," and each sans serif is "a," which makes this sequence babaa aabab aabab. Then looking at the Bacon alphabet, we see that babaa = W, aabab = F, and aabab again = F. So "Knowledge Is Power" spells out WFF, or William F. Friedman's initials.

After William's death, Elizebeth spent the rest of her life archiving his work and their collection of cryptographic books, creating the biggest private collection of works on codes and ciphers. The collection is now housed in the George C. Marshall Research Library in Lexington, Virginia. Much of Elizebeth's government work remained classified until quite recently, meaning it was so secret, the public couldn't read about it. Colonel Rose Mary Sheldon, an intelligence expert at the Virginia Military Institute, said, "We know she was involved in the [Office of Strategic Services], we know that one of their biggest cases was broken because of her, but we can't seem to declassify or find evidence of what she did."

In 1957, the NSA confiscated stacks of material from Elizebeth's collection, reclassifying it from "restricted" to "confidential." Years before his death, articles and lectures that William himself had written were considered "too secret" for him to own any longer. The NSA took more documents in the 1970s and 1980s but was forced by the Freedom of Information Act to return more than 10,000 items in the 1990s. These are all part of the archive Elizebeth gave to the George C. Marshall Research Library. The evidence for her achievements lies in the vast archive she herself built.

In 1975, the NSA named the main auditorium in their Fort Meade campus after William Friedman. Women working at the NSA pushed to have Elizebeth's name included. In the 1990s, with the release of her documents and proof of her work, it finally was. Elizebeth and William are now recognized together as the two most influential code-breakers in American history.

We still don't know Elizebeth's full story, but her most important achievements are clear. The young, seemingly insignificant girl from Indiana became one of the best code-breakers of all time. She cracked the toughest codes during two world wars, as well as during the bloody decade of major crime spurred by Prohibition. Elizebeth's passion for the truth and her drive to discover it in all its forms led her from Shakespeare to bootleggers to spymasters. She took her "marvelous abilities" and used them in ways nobody could have imagined that long-ago day when she walked into the Newberry Library in Chicago.

Elizebeth working at her desk, 1940 *(George C. Marshall Foundation)*

AUTHOR'S NOTE

I was drawn to Elizebeth's story because she had clearly achieved so much and yet in death, as in life, she remained in her husband's shadows. Even the recorded interviews with her that are housed in the George C. Marshall Research Library are really about her husband, William. She is asked about him and his work far more than she is about her own life. What we hear about her is incidental to the main thrust of the questions. As Elizebeth herself wryly noted, people who wanted access to her husband's brain ended up coming to her.

William's achievements are certainly impressive, but as he himself would say, Elizebeth was his equal in every way. Her called her a "remarkable woman." When the rumor spread that she had taught him everything he knew, he agreed. "When people introduce me and then say that my wife is also etc & is really better at it, I invariably assent, with a real smile." They were truly an amazing couple and helped each other become master code-breakers, the very best in their field. After Elizebeth's death at age eighty-eight on October 31, 1980, her ashes were scattered on William's grave. The two partners were together again at last.

When more files are declassified by the NSA, I hope we can learn the full extent of Elizebeth's talents. For now, though, there's enough to show her brilliance and impressive achievements. Elizebeth has finally come out of the shadows and into the light—not into the glare of the media spotlight she so detested, but into her rightful place in history.

WHAT ARE CODES?
WHAT ARE CIPHERS?

The book discusses a number of codes and ciphers. What is the difference? A cipher uses symbols, letters, or numbers to replace the letters in the original message. A code replaces whole words or phrases, or changes the order of letters. Codes can also be nonverbal, like waving flags or flashing lights. Here's an example of a ladder code. Can you figure it out just by looking at the text?

```
I S N E O D A U L O I K S E U T T
H I S A C E C S T O L E N N B I O
T S A K Y B E E I K S N O S E S N
```

This is called a ladder code because that's how you read it. If you read the letters in the normal way, left to right, top row to bottom row, it looks like nonsense. What if you start from the bottom left to the top and back down again, like going up and down a ladder? What does this sentence say?

A grid code is like a ladder code because it also depends on how the letters are arranged. This looks like nonsense:

T W R D H O O S E R S A

P D E Y A I B I S S U T

But what if you knew that you needed to rearrange these letters into a six-letter by four-letter grid? Then you would have:

T H E P A S

W O R D I S

R O S E B U

D S A Y I T

Can you tell what that says by reading it left to right, top to bottom? Can you see how the code above came from taking these letters and rearranging them to go from top to bottom, left to right?

Another kind of code, used during the American Civil War, is a rail fence cipher. Like the ladder code and the grid code, it's a kind of word shuffling. All the right letters are there but in a confusing order. Here's how you do it:

You need to have a message that has letters adding up to multiples of four, so sixteen, twenty, twenty-four letters total. If you have an odd number, say seventeen or thirty-one, then you have to use "null" letters—letters that your fellow spy will know are placeholders, not actual letters. Perhaps you use "z" for this, a letter unlikely to be part of any real message.

Say your message is "Target is London Bridge." That's twenty letters, so there's no need for a null placeholder. Now arrange the message so that every other letter is slighter lower:

T R E I L N O B I G

A G T S O D N R D E

Copy down the top row: TREILNOBIG

Add the bottom row after the top one: TREILNOBI-GAGTSODNRDE

Now here's where the multiple of four thing comes in. To make this code more complex, you chop it into four-letter groups. Now it reads:

TREI LNOB IGAG TSOD NRDE

If you got this message, how would you figure it out? Not knowing what kind of code it is, it can seem impossible. But once you know it's a rail fence, here is what you do. Take all the letters and put them into one long string, but put a marker halfway. In this case after the first ten letters, since there are twenty total:

TREILNOBIG // AGTSODNRDE

Now you see how to re-create the rail fence. The left side letters are the top part of the fence. The right side are the bottom part. You just draw the fence again. And read it by going up and down, left to right. It's true, you can't tell where the word breaks are, but if you space out the letters, your mind will find the words for you:

T A R G E T I S L O N D O N B R I D G E

Now solve this one and see what your brain tells you the words are:

ATCA DWTA KTAN

Even if you didn't know this was a rail fence cipher, you might find this one easy to decode. If you're at war, you can guess that this would be a message about a battle plan or enemy capabilities. Just looking at the letters, there's one mixed-up word that jumps out at you, just as Elizebeth described. Have you found it?

The word is "ATTACK." From that one word, Elizebeth would be able to find the rest.

Anagrams are another simple kind of code that shuffles letter order. Instead of writing "Top Secret," you could write "Pto Rcetes" or "Pot Screet."

Here is a typical code used in the Great War (later known as World War I). It's a key code, meaning you need to have the key to read any messages in it. The key is created by lining up five letters on top, the same five on the side, and filling in the alphabet inside the grid. Since there are twenty-six letters in the alphabet, not twenty-five, the letter "y" is left out. If you need it for your message, you can use "i" instead.

```
      B  L  Q  W  J
  B |K  A  Z  N  W
  L |F  J  Q  R  E
  Q |B  P  U  T  M
  W |H  S  X  C  G
  J |I  L  O  V  D
```

To encode, you use pairs of letters, one from the side of the grid and one from the top, to get to the letter you want. So BB = K, BL = A, BQ = Z, and so on. Knowing that, what does this message spell out?

QW WB LJ WW JQ BW QW BL WW QW JB WL LL JQ BW

To make things really confusing, you can divide the letters up into groups of five (the groups of two are a clue that this is a key-grid code). Then you would have:

QWWBL JWWJQ BWQWB LWWQW JBWLL LJQBW.

This message evenly divides into five-letter groups, but if it didn't, you could add *Y*s as your null letters since there are no *Y*s in the grid.

Another tricky code used during World War I relied on a random key that would change every day. The key would be a string of numbers, for example: 4457900023784. The message would also be a series of numbers, this time presented in an easy way: A = 01, B = 02, C = 03, all the way to Z = 26. If your message is PEARL HARBOR, then first you turn those letters into a string of numbers:

1605011812080118021518

Then you put the random key under it (if your message is longer than the key, just repeat the key) and add the two numbers, not carrying any tens, so 8 + 5 = 3, not 13.

1605011812080118021518

44579000237844445790002

5052911835764553711510

That total number is a cryptogram and what you would send as your secret message. The solver takes the number, subtracts the key from it, and gets your original string of numbers, which can then be easily turned back into the alphabet. Try making up one of your own!

THE BACONIAN CIPHER

This is the Bacon cipher that Elizabeth Wells Gallup believed would prove that Francis Bacon was the author of the plays attributed to William Shakespeare.

a = capital letters (or serif), b = lowercase letters (or sans serif)

A = aaaaa	F = aabab	L = ababa	Q = abbbb	V = baabb
B = aaaab	G = aabba	M = ababb	R = baaaa	W = babaa
C = aaaba	H = aabbb	N = abbaa	S = baaab	X = babab
D = aaabb	I, J = abaaa	O = abbab	T = baaba	Y = babba
E = aabaa	K = abaab	P = abbba	U = baabb	Z = babbb

KnOwl = babaa = W   spOWE = aabab = F

edGeI = aabab = F   r = null letter

THE ZIMMERMAN TELEGRAM

The telegram sent in 1917 by Arthur Zimmerman, a diplomat in the German Embassy in Washington, DC, to the German ambassador in Mexico. British intelligence intercepted the message, which immediately aroused suspicion since it contained no words but only a series of numbers. *(National Archives)*

TELEGRAM RECEIVED.

CLASS... CANCELLED
...ter 1-8-58
...erson, State Dept.

By *Much G Eckoff Antiwest*

Date *Oct. 27, 195?*

FROM 2nd from London # 5747.

"We intend to begin on the first of February unrestricted submarine warfare. We shall endeavor in spite of this to keep the United States of America neutral. In the event of this not succeeding, we make Mexico a proposal of alliance on the following basis: make war together, make peace together, generous financial support and an understanding on our part that Mexico is to reconquer the lost territory in Texas, New Mexico, and Arizona. The settlement in detail is left to you. You will inform the President of the above most secretly as soon as the outbreak of war with the United States of America is certain and add the suggestion that he should, on his own initiative, *invite* ~~invite~~ Japan to immediate adherence and at the same time mediate between Japan and ourselves. Please call the President's attention to the fact that the ruthless employment of our submarines now offers the prospect of compelling England in a few months to make peace." Signed, ZIMMERMANN.

The Zimmerman telegram decryption *(National Archives)*

THE VOYNICH MANUSCRIPT

The pages below and at right are from the Voynich Manuscript, a fifteenth-century codex, by an unknown author
and written in an unknown script. The manuscript con-
sists of 240 colorfully illustrated pages, but there appear
to be pages missing. A single manuscript page measures
approximately 6½ x 9⅓ inches (16.5 x 23.7 cm).

William tried for years to solve the code in its pages.
Elizebeth helped for a while but left the project to William. To this day, it remains a mystery. The manuscript
is named after Wilfrid Voynich, a Polish-Lithuanian
book dealer who purchased it in 1912. Since 1969, it has
been held in Yale University's Beinecke Rare Book and
Manuscript Library.

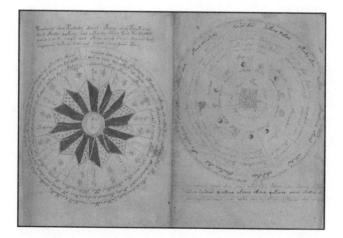

Above: Page 88 from the Voynich Manuscript *(Bienecke Rare Book Collection, Yale University)*

Left: Pages 67 and 68 from the Voynich Manuscript *(Bienecke Rare Book Collection, Yale University)*

GLOSSARY

anagram: A word made by jumbling the letters of original word into a new order.

anti-Semitism: Hatred toward Jewish people, considering them inferior to other people.

Bacon, Sir Francis: English philosopher and statesman who was Lord Chancellor under King James I. His writings are about the scientific method, using observation and inferences to understand the world.

Becker, Johannes Siegfried: Code-named "Sargo," Becker was the principal agent organizing a ring of Nazi agents. His ring's primary focus at first was sabotage, especially of ships. Later, the plan shifted to coups for replacing unfriendly South American governments with ones sympathetic to Germany.

cipher: A way of writing secret messages using symbols, letters, or numbers to replace the letters in the original message.

code: A way of sending secret messages by replacing whole words or phrases or changing the order of letters. Codes can also be nonverbal, like waving flags or flashing lights.

cryptanalysis: The study of ciphers and codes.

cryptanalyst: A person who studies ciphers and codes.

cryptology: The art of writing and solving codes.

decipherment: The solving of ciphers.

decryption: The decoding of data, of a message.

eccentric: oddball, strange.

encryption: The process of putting a message into a code or cipher.

Engels, Gustav Albrecht: Code-named "Alfredo," Engels was recruited by the Abwehr in 1939 to provide economic intelligence. This role expanded to include all areas, and by mid-1941, Engels was passing along information on production and military movements in the United States, as well as in Brazil.

folio: An old-fashioned kind of book made of large, folded sheets of paper.

Franczok, Wolf: Code-named "Luna," Franczok worked for the Abwehr with Engels and Becker as a radio engineer, setting up radio stations and Enigma machines throughout South America.

Reichsmark: German money during the Third Reich, under Hitler's government.

reverse engineering: Deconstructing how something is built to figure out how it works. By looking at a product, figuring out the machine that created it.

sans serif: A plain typeface with no little lines attached to the letters: This font is sans serif.

serif: A typeface with little lines attached to the letters. **This font is serif.**

Shakespeare, William: English poet, playwright, and actor, active in the late 1500s and early 1600s. The most famous writer in England.

suffragette: A woman advocating and protesting for the right to vote, active in the early twentieth century.

TIMELINE

September 24, 1891: Wolf (William) Friedman born in Chişinău, Bessarabia, the son of Romanian Jews.

August 26, 1892: Elizebeth Smith born in Huntington, Indiana, to John Marion Smith, a Quaker dairyman, and Sophia Smith. She was the youngest of nine surviving children (a tenth child died very early).

1911–1913: Elizebeth attends the University of Wooster in Ohio.

1913: Elizebeth transfers to Hillsdale College in Michigan to be closer to her sick mother.

Summer 1915: Elizebeth graduates college with honors, getting a degree in English literature, having studied Latin, Greek, and German. Only she and one other sibling go to college, and she pays her own way, having borrowed money from her father at 6 percent interest. Elizebeth repays the loan.

Fall 1915: Elizebeth gets a job as a substitute principal at a public high school in Wabash, Indiana.

Elizebeth and Fabyan at Riverbank, 1916 *(George C. Marshall Foundation)*

Spring 1916: Elizebeth quits the job and goes to Chicago in search of a new position.

1916: Elizebeth takes a job with George Fabyan, living and working at his Riverbank estate outside of Chicago. Her task is to crack the cipher proving that Francis Bacon was the real author of Shakespeare's plays and sonnets. She meets William F. Friedman, a biologist assigned to photograph folio pages to help the cipher-solvers.

1916–1920: Elizebeth works with Friedman at the Riverbank Cipher School, cracking codes for the War Department in the run-up to the United States entering the Great War, later called World War I, and after entry into the war.

April 1917: The United States declares war on Germany, entering the Great War. The United States, Britain, France, Russia, and Italy are allies fighting Germany, Austria-Hungary, the Ottoman Empire, and Bulgaria.

May 1917: Elizebeth marries William Friedman. She is happy to take his last name, having always felt that "Smith" was the most boring last name possible.

1917: A detective from Scotland Yard brings a briefcase full of coded messages for Elizebeth and William to solve. Hindu separatists are organizing with Germans to fight British control of India. They use a book code.

1917–1920: Elizebeth and William publish eight pamphlets on code-cracking using Riverbank's vanity press. The couple writes the pamphlets together, calls them "our pamphlets,"

Elizebeth and William, newlyweds at Riverbank, 1917 *(George C. Marshall Foundation)*

but Elizebeth's name is listed on only two of them. Fabyan registers the copyright under his own name, something that Elizebeth makes sure is later corrected.

1918: William enlists in the US Army Signal Corps, serving in France as personal cryptographer for General John Pershing.

November 11, 1918: Germany surrenders, end of World War I.

1919: William returns from military service. Couple returns to Riverbank.

January 17, 1920: Prohibition begins. Production, transportation, and sales of alcohol are now illegal in the United States. Consumption, however, is legal.

1920: Elizebeth and William accept a job offer from the Army, working with the Signal Corps.

1921: Elizebeth and William move to Washington, DC, to start work together for the War Department. William starts to study machines used for enciphering messages. The Enigma machine is one of them, a typewriter-like machine developed by a young German in 1918. William is impressed but considers the machine not secure enough. He develops his own version, the SIGABA machine, during the 1920s, an unbreakable cipher machine.

1922: Elizebeth leaves the Signal Corps. She writes books on codes for children.

A type of Enigma machine. The cipher device was developed and used in the early- to mid-twentieth century to protect communication by Nazi Germany during World War II. (*Photo courtesy of Robert Scheifer: Bletchley Park.*)

1923: The couple's first child is born, a daughter named Barbara. Elizebeth develops code for a wealthy businessman, Edward McLean, to keep his correspondence secret.

1923: Elizebeth is hired to work as cryptanalyst for the Navy. Her task finished, she resigns after six months.

1924: The US Treasury hires Elizebeth to crack smugglers' codes for the Coast Guard. She works from home and is given the title "special agent, US Treasury." In the first three months, she solves the backlog of the past two years.

1926: The couple's second child is born, a son named John.

July 1931: Elizebeth is allowed to build her own team. Three men and two women work under her. Now she has an office, a pay raise, and a new title: cryptanalyst-in-charge. She continues her work for the US Coast Guard and Treasury Department, solving coded and enciphered messages sent by criminals and smugglers. She testifies in many high-profile cases, securing convictions with her convincing testimony. She also keeps a record of every code and cipher solved, compiling the information into thirty books by the end of the year.

December 5, 1933: Prohibition is repealed, being a colossal failure as a law but a big success in encouraging criminal mafias to traffic illegal substances.

1937: The Canadian government asks for Elizebeth's help cracking the codes of a Chinese opium dealer. Despite not knowing Chinese, she solves the complicated cipher code,

Friedman family, December 5, 1933 *(George C. Marshall Foundation)*

and her work results in the conviction of the leader of the gang, as well as of others.

1938: Elizebeth works for the Coast Guard, focusing on enemy spies spying on the United States, especially Germans in Latin America. William, meanwhile, stays with the Navy and works on cracking Purple, the Japanese Enigma machine.

September 1, 1939: Nazi Germany invades Poland. World War II starts as France and England declare war on Germany in response. Later Japan and Italy join Germany, forming the Axis. The Soviet Union, China, and ultimately the United States join France and England, forming the Allies.

January 1940: Elizebeth decodes messages revealing Hitler's preparations to invade Scandinavia, as well as information about British ships.

September 1940: The London Blitz begins, the German bombing of the British capital. For nearly two years, wave after wave of German planes drop bombs on London and other major English and Scottish cities, killing close to 40,000 civilians, wounding another 25,000, and destroying or damaging more than a million homes.

September 1940: William cracks the Purple code. He builds replicas of the cipher machine to give to British intelligence at Bletchley Park and General Douglas MacArthur in the Philippines.

January 4, 1941: William suffers a nervous breakdown and is hospitalized for ten weeks. Doctors diagnose him as having

Barbara and John, circa 1930s *(George C. Marshall Foundation)*

an "anxiety reaction" brought on by the stress of intense work on a top-secret project. When William is discharged in March, he is given an honorable discharge, losing military rank and status. He continues his cryptography work as a civilian. Years later, he sues to regain his rank.

July 1941: Elizebeth is assigned to create an "independent code room and message center" for the new Office of Strategic Services (OSS), led by William Donovan.

November 1941: After a German U-boat sinks an American ship, killing more than one hundred sailors, President Roosevelt signs an executive order placing the Coast Guard under the control of the Navy rather than the Treasury Department. Elizebeth's unit is now under Navy control. Using an old Enigma machine from 1918, she and her team have cracked the new Enigma machine codes used by the Nazis to communicate with their agents in South America.

December 7, 1941: Japan attacks Pearl Harbor in Hawaii. Two thousand Americans are killed, twenty-one ships sunk, almost two hundred planes destroyed, a large part of the Pacific Fleet.

December 8, 1941: America declares war on Japan. Germany declares war on America.

December 1941: Elizebeth is moved to US Coast Guard Unit 387, under the Navy, and tasked with solving coded messages between South America and Nazi Germany. She hears a lot of chatter about American and British ships, targets of German U-boat attacks. In 1942 alone, 1,027 ships are torpedoed and sunk by German submarines. Elizebeth quickly cracks two of the German Enigma codes, the Blue and the Green, the Abwehr and the Embassy messages. Bletchley Park cracks these Enigma codes around the same time.

January 1942: Elizebeth's unit agrees to share information with the British Radio Intelligence Service.

February 1942: The Coast Guard stops passing on decrypted messages to the FBI due to the agency's careless handling of intelligence. The FBI had admitted to releasing information about Allied ships' status that had allowed the Germans to attack and sink the vessels. Plus, while the Coast Guard had been sharing information, the FBI had not been doing the same.

March 18, 1942: Pressured by the FBI, Brazilian police arrest German spies and agents. Enigma codes are changed.

April 1942: Meeting of high-level cryptographers from the United States, Canada, and England. Elizebeth is the only woman included. The FBI is pointedly left out.

February 1943: Becker moves the Nazi spy ring headquarters to Paraguay, then Buenos Aires, Argentina.

May 1943: Luna sets up a new radio network for Nazi agents, communicating between South America and Germany.

1943: Elizebeth cracks the new Enigma codes. She shares the information with British intelligence, and they all agree to give the FBI only general summaries of information rather than decrypted messages.

Codenamed Purple by the United States, a Japanese encryption machine used from February 1939 to the end of World War II *(Photo courtesy of Robert Scheifer: Bletchley Park)*

June 4, 1943: Generals in Argentina, supported by Nazi agents, stage a coup. The new president is Pedro Pablo Ramírez, but the real power is held by Juan Perón, who has close ties with the Nazis.

July 1943: Elizebeth's unit grows to twenty-three people, still tiny in comparison to William's—or to Bletchley Park.

Fall 1943: Hoover realizes that he isn't getting decrypted messages anymore from the Coast Guard and threatens to shut down Elizebeth's unit. He complains to the head of the Navy, Rear Admiral Schuirman. The admiral defends the Coast Guard and assures the FBI that the intelligence is being appropriately handled. He adds that if the FBI compromises the unit's work by talking to the Argentine authorities and revealing the messages being read, the agency will seriously harm the war effort. Hoover bitterly complains but backs down.

October 2, 1943: Osmar Hellmuth, an Argentine naval officer, is named consul to Barcelona to provide diplomatic cover for his mission. He sets sail to Germany to get weapons for use in planned coups across South America. When his ship stops for refueling at Trinidad, he is secretly taken by the British. Once they find the incriminating weapons list and instructions, Hellmuth loses all diplomatic privileges. He quickly confesses the extent of the plots, naming every name he knows.

November 1943: The network of German agents in South America is ready to start a series of coups. They plan to ensure new governments will be sympathetic to the Nazi cause.

December 20, 1943: Bolivia's government falls in a successful coup.

January 1944: The Argentine government arrests some German and Spanish spies, sending Sargo and Luna into hiding. For a while, there is radio silence, but the two agents start up again, though not at the same level as earlier.

January 26, 1944: Confronted with Hellmuth's confession of Argentine support of the Nazis, Argentina is forced by the Allies to cut off all ties to Germany or be considered an enemy.

February 1944: Elizebeth cracks the last Enigma code, the Red code for the SS. Her unit sends the news to Bletchley Park, offering to wire details of the solution. The British at Bletchley crack the code at the same time and respond, "details not required."

March 25, 1944: William is awarded the Exceptional Service Medal, the War Department's highest honor, by General Harry Fugles.

August 18, 1944: Luna, a radio operator, one of the last two Nazi agents in Argentina, and a principal mastermind behind the spy mission in South America, is arrested.

April 19, 1945: Sargo, a.k.a. Becker, is arrested in Buenos Aires, the last Nazi agent and the main figure behind the entire German spy ring. Becker talks freely about the support given by Perón in Argentina and the plans to take over the continent.

TIMELINE

April 30, 1945: Hitler kills himself in an underground bunker.

May 8, 1945: With Germany's surrender, the war in Europe is over.

September 1, 1945: With Japan's surrender, the war in the Pacific is over.

1945: William is sent to Europe to sweep up intelligence material. He ends his tour in England, at Bletchley Park, meeting with Alan Turing and top Nazi cryptologists imprisoned there.

February 1946: Spruille Braden, America's assistant secretary of state, publishes a "Blue Book" detailing evidence of Perón's ties to the Nazis. Perón responds by accusing Braden himself of being the head of a vast spy network in South America. He goes on to accuse Braden of extorting money from Argentine businessmen to finance his political campaign.

February 1946: Juan Perón is elected president of Argentina. He offers his country as a safe refuge for any and all Nazis, including those guilty of war crimes.

September 12, 1946: Elizebeth leaves the Coast Guard, having recommended that her unit be shut down. She has talked herself out of a job.

1947: Elizebeth works for the International Monetary Fund (IMF), creating and managing secure communications.

1949: William is named head of the cryptographic division of the Armed Forces Security Agency (AFSA).

1952: William is made chief cryptologist for the National Security Agency (NSA), a new organization growing out of AFSA. He writes a series of textbooks to train new agents for the NSA.

October 12, 1955: William is awarded the National Security Medal by Allan Dulles.

1956: William retires. Elizebeth and William write *The Shakespearean Ciphers Examined*, debunking the idea of a code embedded in the plays to prove Francis Bacon's authorship of the works.

1957: The NSA comes to Elizebeth and William's home to seize material they have reclassified as too secret for them to own (including papers they themselves had written). They take forty-eight items.

Fall 1957: The book is published with the title *Ciphers Examined* by Cambridge University Press and wins awards from the Folger Shakespeare Library and the American Shakespeare Theatre.

November 12, 1969: William dies and is buried in Arlington Cemetery. His grave marker is his final code.

1970: Elizebeth donates the cryptographic library she and William had spent their life compiling to the George C. Marshall Research Library in Lexington, Virginia.

1975: The NSA comes to the George C. Marshall Research Library to seize more material from Elizebeth and William's collection. The NSA names the main auditorium on their Fort Meade campus in William Friedman's honor.

TIMELINE

October 31, 1980: Elizebeth dies. Her ashes are scattered around her husband's grave, and her name is added to his headstone.

1983: The Freedom of Information Act is used to force the NSA to release more than 10,000 items taken from Elizebeth and William's archive. All the material is given back to the George C. Marshall Research Library.

1999: Elizebeth is inducted into the NSA Hall of Honor.

2002: NSA's OPS1 building is dedicated to Elizebeth and William Friedman during the NSA's Fiftieth Anniversary Commemoration.

April 2019: US Senate passes a resolution honoring the life and legacy of Elizebeth Smith Friedman, cryptanalyst.

NOTES

CHAPTER ONE

8   "PLEASE COOPERATE," Jason Fagone, *The Woman Who Smashed Codes* (New York: HarperCollins, 2017), 169.

9   "I'll confess, Mrs. Friedman," interview with Margaret Santry, NBC radio, May 25, 1934, George C. Marshall Library.

9   "I never thought," interview with Santry, May 25, 1934.

10   "Ad absurdum!" Fagone, *The Woman Who Smashed Codes*, 169.

10   "After those," Stuart Smith, *A Life in Code: Pioneer Cryptanalyst Elizebeth Smith Friedman* (Jefferson, NC: McFarland, 2017), 50.

CHAPTER 2

12   "My professors told me," Fagone, *The Woman Who Smashed Codes*, 9.

12   "I have marvelous abilities, yet do not use them," Fagone, *The Woman Who Smashed Codes*, 9.

14   "restless mental question mark," Fagone, *The Woman Who Smashed Codes*, 9.

15   "we glide over," *The Woman Who Smashed Codes*, 6.

16   "I am never quite so gleeful as when I am doing something labeled as an 'ought not.' . . . I should have been born a man," Fagone, *The Woman Who Smashed Codes*, 10.

17   "any nearer to me than the moon," Elizebeth Smith Friedman, unpublished memoir, George C. Marshall Research Library archive, Lexington, VA, 1.

17   "that an archaeologist would have, when he suddenly realized after years of digging that he was inside the tomb of a great pharaoh," Friedman, unpublished memoir, 1.

18   "He wasted no time . . . and [to] spend the night," Friedman, unpublished memoir, 2.

18   "but he was the kind of man who did not take no for an answer," Friedman, unpublished memoir, 2.

19   "probably appeared a demure," Friedman, unpublished memoir, 3.

19   "WHAT DO YOU KNOW?" June 4, 1974, interview, George C. Marshall Foundation.

20   "That remains, sir, for *you* to find out," June 4, 1974, interview, 17.

CHAPTER 3

21 "I'm spending money to discover valuable things that universities can't afford. You can never get sick of too much knowledge," Fagone, *The Woman Who Smashed Codes*, 25.

23 "real aristocrat," June 4, 1974, interview .

27 "wasn't really sincere," June 4, 1974, interview .

28 "a matter of what is properly," June 4, 1974, interview .

CHAPTER 4

31 "sliding strip cipher her husband had developed": This cipher is identical to one developed by Thomas Jefferson, though it was not discovered in his papers until after World War I.

CHAPTER 5

35 "The skeletons of words leap out and make you jump," Fagone, *The Woman Who Smashed Codes*, 75.

39 "considerable regret," Fagone, *The Woman Who Smashed Codes*, 26.

39 "since we had completed," Fagone, *The Woman Who Smashed Codes*, 26.

CHAPTER 6

41 "He gave orders," Friedman, unpublished memoir, 9.

42   "He was gentle," Friedman, unpublished memoir, 13.

CHAPTER 7

48   "Would you lean back," June 4, 1974, interview.

48   "All right, I'm ready," June 4, 1974, interview.

50   "I, a mere woman," Fagone, *The Woman Who Smashed Codes*, 103.

51   "I am inclined to agree," Fagone, *The Woman Who Smashed Codes*, 111.

52   "Days, weeks, and months," Friedman, unpublished memoir, 46.

53   *The Index of Coincidence*: If you take any two lines of English text, one above the other, there will be places where the same letters line up vertically. Friedman found that this happens in roughly seven columns out of every one hundred, or about 7 percent of the time. This "index of coincidence" differs in each language. We can use the index of coincidence to create ciphers, employing the same key for sender and recipient, though the sender will have an enciphered message starting at a different place in the key each time. The recipient would know where to start by some previous agreement and then place the messages one above the other and slide them back and forth until the right vertical fit is found. Once correctly aligned,

each letter in the vertical column has been enciphered with the same key letter as all the other letters in that column.

CHAPTER 8

55 "as powerful as he is ruthless," Fagone, *The Woman Who Smashed Codes*, 113.

55 "Fabyan accepted his fate," Friedman, unpublished memoir, 48.

56 "By the end of the war," Friedman, unpublished memoir, 114.

56 "made a reputation," Friedman, unpublished memoir, 115.

57 "Miss Transposition," Friedman, unpublished memoir, 128.

57 "Miss Substitution," Friedman, unpublished memoir, 128.

57 "This was a case," Friedman, unpublished memoir, 54.

CHAPTER 9

62 "and when they couldn't," June 5, 1974, interview, George C. Marshall Foundation.

65   "I went here, there, and everywhere," Fagone, *The Woman Who Smashed Codes*, 127–28.

65   "It scared me," Smith, *A Life in Code*, 50.

CHAPTER 10

69   "EFBS NPUIFS BOE EFBS EBEEZ": deciphered as DEAR MOTHER AND DEAR DADDY, George C. Marshall Foundation.

CHAPTER 11

71   "was reported to be very common in the halls of Congress," Friedman, unpublished memoir, 61.

71   "a jury itself was tried for drinking up the evidence," Friedman, unpublished memoir, 68.

72   "Al Capone was said," June 5, 1974, interview.

74   "I must declare," June 5, 1974, interview.

75   "very mean mood," Fagone, *The Woman Who Smashed Codes*, 139.

75   "Key woman of the T-men," Smith, *A Life in Code*, 50.

76   "a pretty young woman," Friedman, unpublished memoir, 88.

76   "One of the fictions," Friedman, unpublished memoir, 85.

76   "I know how much," Fagone, *The Woman Who Smashed Codes*, 172.

77   "Dad used to joke," Smith, *A Life in Code*, 106.

77   "own indomitable spirit," Smith, *A Life in Code*, 153.

CHAPTER 12

80   "about the most disreputable," June 5, 1974, interview.

82   "I pack my bag," Friedman, unpublished memoir, 100.

82   "We have to keep," Fagone, *The Woman Who Smashed Codes*, 167.

82   "The mystery-lure," Fagone, *The Woman Who Smashed Codes*, 167.

83   "I argued to myself," June 5, 1974, interview.

84   "in careers unusual," Fagone, *The Woman Who Smashed Codes*, 169.

CHAPTER 13

88   "the spy stuff!" Friedman, unpublished memoir, 97.

88   "a vast dome of silence," Fagone, *The Woman Who Smashed Codes*, 176.

88   "the fame of Mrs. Friedman," Smith, *A Life in Code*, 106.

88   "It is a hodge-podge," Smith, *A Life in Code*, 106.

89   "I'm angry enough," Smith, *A Life in Code*, 108.

89 "exciting, round-the-clock adventures," in unpublished "footnote to history" by Elizebeth Smith Friedman, George C. Marshall Library, 108.

91 "It gets mixed up," May 16, 1973, interview, George C. Marshall Library.

CHAPTER 14

93 "Look, this group," May 16, 1973, interview.

94 "He didn't mention," May 16, 1973, interview.

95 "He had done something," Smith, *A Life in Code*, 111.

95 "makeshift machine," May 16, 1973, interview.

95 "They were gone long before," Smith, *A Life in Code*, 142.

95 "Sometimes I'd awaken," Smith, *A Life in Code*, 142.

96 "reason of physical," Smith, *A Life in Code*, 111.

99 "The FBI exposed," Fagone, *The Woman Who Smashed Codes*, 234.

CHAPTER 15

100 "ought not," Fagone, *The Woman Who Smashed Codes*, 9.

103 "someone inside the office," Smith, *A Life in Code*, 103.

103 "Any South American country," Fagone, *The Woman Who Smashed Codes*, 218.

CHAPTER 16

108 "Try with all means," Smith, *A Life in Code*, 132.

109 "urgent need," Fagone, *The Woman Who Smashed Codes*, 240.

111 "But they knew," *The Woman Who Smashed Codes*, 237.

112 "cryptologic schizophrenia," Fagone, *The Woman Who Smashed Codes*, 237.

113 "like saying he had," *The Friedman Legacy*, Center for Cryptologic History, National Security Agency, 2006, 175.

113 "only confuse," *The Friedman Legacy*, 175.

CHAPTER 17

116 "measures against members," Fagone, *The Woman Who Smashed Codes*, 241–42.

CHAPTER 18

122 "it would be more suitable," *The Friedman Legacy*, 133.

123 "I fear that MEYER," Fagone, *The Woman Who Smashed Codes*, 245.

124 "Take all precautionary measures," Fagone, *The Woman Who Smashed Codes*, 247.

CHAPTER 19

131 "evidence that Perón," Friedman, unpublished memoir, 97.

132 "Final objective," Fagone, *The Woman Who Smashed Codes*, 274.

CHAPTER 20

138 "details not required," Fagone, *The Woman Who Smashed Codes*, 286.

CHAPTER 21

140 "there is a leak," Smith, *A Life in Code*, 286.

140 "Operation concerning unrest," Smith, *A Life in Code*, 286.

142 "The ability to read," Smith, *A Life in Code*, 139.

CHAPTER 22

146 "Common practice," Smith, *A Life in Code*, 151.

147 "This is somewhat belated," *A Life in Code*, 151.

151 "The indictment," Smith, *A Life in Code*, 158.

CHAPTER 23

154 "mention of contact with any political," *The Politics of Espionage*, 380.

CHAPTER 25

165   "We know she was involved," Smith, *A Life in Code*, 11.

AUTHOR'S NOTE

169   "remarkable woman," Fagone, *The Woman Who Smashed Codes*, 153.

169   "When people," Fagone, *The Woman Who Smashed Codes*, 169.

SELECTED BIBLIOGRAPHY

Elements of Cryptanalysis, Training Pamphlet No. 3, prepared
in the Office of the Chief Signal Officer, May 1923,
Washington Government Printing Office. Course given
by Capt. W. F. Friedman.

Fagone, Jason. *The Woman Who Smashed Codes*. New York:
HarperCollins, 2017.

Friedman, Elizebeth. Unpublished memoir, footnote to history,
and oral interviews from 1934, 1973, 1974, archived in
the George C. Marshall Research Library, Lexington, VA.

German Clandestine Activities in South America in World War II,
United States Cryptologic History, series 4, World War
II, volume 3, National Security Agency, Central Security
Service, declassified and approved for release on April 13,
2009.

Kahn, David. *The Codebreakers*. New York: Scribner, 1967.

SELECTED BIBLIOGRAPHY

McGaha, Richard. *The Politics of Espionage: Nazi Diplomats and Spies in Argentina, 1933–1945*. PhD dissertation, College of Arts and Sciences of Ohio University, November 2009.

Pincock, Stephan. *Codebreaker*. New York: Walker & Co., 2006.

Smith, G. Stuart. *A Life in Code: Pioneer Cryptanalyst Elizabeth Smith Friedman*. Jefferson, NC: McFarland, 2017.

The Friedman Legacy: A Tribute to William and Elizabeth Friedman, Sources in Cryptologic History, Number 3, Center for Cryptologic History, National Security Agency, 2006.

Wrixon, Fred. *Codes, Ciphers, and Secret Languages*. New York: Bonanza Books, 1989.

ACKNOWLEDGMENTS

Every book is a journey and for this one, I'd like to thank my long-time editor Howard Reeves, who always offers important insights and comments. Every writer needs a good editor, and I'm fortunate to have Howard helping me to shape each story into the best form it can take. Thanks, too, to assistant editor Sara Sproull for her efficiency and organization, always keeping me on track. And thanks to assistant art director Heather Kelly, managing editor Amy Vreeland, and associate production director Erin Vandeveer, as well as all the other people at Abrams who shepherd my books out into the world and into the hands of readers.

I'm fortunate to have a truly exceptional writers' group, whose keen eyes on these pages have offered invaluable critiques. Gennifer Choldenko, Diane Fraser, Betsy Partridge, Emily Polsby, and Pam Turner have all improved these pages.

And finally, thanks to the archivists and librarians who helped me sift through archival material and find what I needed. Libraries and librarians are a writer's best friends.

INDEX

INDEX

INDEX